Helen McNeil was born in ▮▮▮▮ in ▮▮▮▮ KT-519-934 After taking her B.A. further west at Reed College, Oregon, she did her doctorate in English at Yale University, writing a dissertation on Wallace Stevens. Since 1972 she has been a Lecturer in the School of English and American Studies at the University of East Anglia, where she teaches American litera- ture, Film Studies and Women's Studies. She has written numerous articles and reviews, and broadcasts on these topics regularly on Radio 3 and 4. She is a member of the Virago Press Advisory Group. Helen McNeil is married to the sculptor Graham Ashton and has two children; she divides her time between Norwich and London.

Virago Pioneers are important reassessments of the lives and ideas of women from every walk of life and all periods of history, re-evaluating their contribution in the light of work done over the past twenty years or more — work that has led to important changes of perspective on women's place in history and contemporary life.

Forthcoming Pioneers

Teresa of Avila
Leonie Caldecott

Ada Lovelace
Rachel Garden

Emily Brontë
Janet Rée

Margaret MacMillan
Carolyn Steedman

Willa Cather
Hermione Lee

Florence Nightingale
Margaret Walters

Jane Digby
Rana Kabbani

Eva Peron
Maxine Molyneux

Eleonora Duse
Eleanor Bron

Sappho
Margaret Williamson

George Eliot
Jennifer Uglow

Queen Victoria
Dorothy Thompson

Thérèse of Lisieux
Monica Furlong

Mary Wollstonecraft
Barbara Taylor

EMILY DICKINSON

Helen McNeil

Published by VIRAGO PRESS Limited
41 William IV Street, London WC2N 4DB

Copyright © Helen McNeil 1986

All rights reserved

Quotations from Emily Dickinson's poems are by permission
of the publishers from *The Poems of Emily Dickinson*, Thomas
H. Johnson ed., Cambridge, Mass.; Harvard University Press,
© 1951, 1955, 1979, 1983 by the President and Fellows of
Harvard College. Quotations from *The Complete Poems of
Emily Dickinson*, Thomas H. Johnson, ed., © 1914, 1929,
1935, 1942 by Martha Dickinson Bianchi; © renewed 1957,
1963 by Mary L. Hampson. Reprinted by permission of Little,
Brown & Co.

British Library Cataloguing in Publication Data
McNeil, Helen
     Emily Dickinson. — (Virago pioneers)
     1. Dickinson, Emily — Criticism and interpretation
     I. Title
     811'.4   PS1541.Z5

     ISBN 0−86068−619−1

Typeset by Florencetype Limited, Bristol
Printed in Great Britain by Anchor Brendon,
Tiptree, Essex

The Inner — paints the Outer —
The Brush without the Hand —

To George and Dora, my father and mother

CONTENTS

viii   *Emily Dickinson*

PREFACE AND ACKNOWLEDGEMENTS

All books are written by many people, but only one person is responsible for the shape the book takes. Emily Dickinson is one of the writers of this book, by her example as well as by her accomplishment. In the course of my work on this study, many other people have inscribed their thoughts and presences on the text. Graham Ashton has turned his intense gaze to my manuscript and to the woman behind it, giving life to both. Ursula Owen of Virago Press has been a model of the supportive editor, even during the 'long foreground' that preceded writing. Professor Richard Sewall gave an earlier version of my conclusion a sympathetic and helpful reading, and a meeting with him saved me many repetitions. Philippa Berry's 'few notes' helped guide some theoretical aspects of the book towards a more generous clarity. Many others, in their very different ways, helped shape the book in its present form. These are: Sara Berschtel of Pantheon Press, Harold Bloom, Thomas Elsaesser, Helene Fesenmaier, Simon Gandolfi, Robert Gross, Jane Havell, Marianne Majerus, and Catherine Monney; also Catherine Itzin and Leslie Saunders of 'The Mothers', our writing group. Liberty and Gabriel, my children, have given more than they take.

The University of East Anglia's termly sabbatical gave me the time for writing, and their enlightened tradition of encouraging faculty members to teach in the area of their current research gave depth to my studies. The students in my seminar on 'The Native Tradition' have shared their considerable insights with me. A small grant some years ago from the British Academy enabled me to begin my researches. A kind invitation by the Department of American Studies and the

Georges Lurcy fund of Amherst College, Massachusetts, resulted in a lecture which developed into Chapters 4 and 5. Daniel Lombardo, Curator of Special Collections at The Jones Library, Amherst, offered informed guidance to the Library's collection and help with photographic reproduction. My thanks to them for permission to use their photograph of Lavinia Dickinson and her cat. I am grateful to the Belknap Press, Harvard University, for permission to reproduce two pages of Emily Dickinson's fair copies of 'Wild Nights – Wild Nights!' and 'They Shut me up in Prose' and the portrait of the Dickinson children.

Throughout this book, certain concerns of feminism, literary analysis, post-structuralism and what one might call the new rhetorical criticism are intermingled, I hope fruitfully. These concerns have quite distinct origins. My treatment of Dickinson's female critique could hardly have taken its present form without the pioneering work of Ellen Moers, Sandra Gilbert and Susan Gubar, and Elaine Showalter, and my last chapter takes its impetus from Paul de Man's humane critique of literary sublimation. Although I doubt many of Jacques Derrida's assertions, I have found his strategic notion of 'difference' a most valuable tool in understanding Dickinson's discontinuities. Much of the biographical information in my study is credited to Richard Sewall's *The Life of Emily Dickinson*, but even more comes from his researches. Of the many critical voices in books on Dickinson, I have found myself conversing most with those of Brita Lindberg-Seyersted, Robert Weisbuch, Margaret Homans, Suzanne Juhasz and Christopher Benfey. My own work has led me to conclude that Dickinson is far less metaphysical and romantic than her mid-century context might imply; the appearance of this non-transcendent Dickinson in articles by Roland Hagenbüchle and E. Miller Budick may indicate the development of a new perspective.

Emily Dickinson tended not to give her poems titles. I have followed her practice, referring to poems by their first lines. If a passage is quoted without other reference, then it begins with the poem's first line. Notes generally refer to books by their short titles, with full publication details being given in the

Bibliography; a few books which are not mentioned elsewhere are given their full publication details in the notes.

Throughout my work, I have been deeply indebted to earlier editors and critics of Dickinson. These debts have been acknowledged at many points in the text. I have, however, wanted this book to be accessible to the general reader as well as to the student or academic specialist. As a result, I have not always referred in the notes to other critics' discussions of a given poem or paused in my argument to elaborate the critical history of a given view. For these sins of omission I hope I may be forgiven. Finally, although many people are inscribed upon this text, only I am responsible for any mistakes in it. I am acutely conscious that recent criticism, including mine, has only barely begun to understand the breadth of Dickinson's accomplishment.

CHRONOLOGY

1830   *10 December:* Emily Dickinson born in Amherst, Mass.; second child, after Austin (1829−95), of lawyer Edward Dickinson and Emily Norcross Dickinson. Dickinsons living in The Homestead, built by Edward's father Samuel Fowler Dickinson.

1833   Lavinia ('Vinnie') Dickinson, sister, born (d. 1899).

1835   Edward Dickinson appointed Treasurer of Amherst College.

1836   Ralph Waldo Emerson (1803−82) publishes essay 'Nature'.

1837   Great Panic; thousands ruined in American business collapse.

1839   Margaret Fuller (1810−50) initiates female intellectual 'conversation' meetings in Boston, which continue until 1844.

1840   Grandfather Dickinson having moved to Ohio, Edward Dickinson sells his half of The Homestead and moves his family to another house in Amherst. Emily and Lavinia enter co-educational Amherst Academy. Emerson publishes *Essays, First Series*, co-founds magazine *The Transcendentalist* (1840−44) with Fuller.

1842   Edward Dickinson elected State Senator in Massachusetts; elected again in 1843.

1845   Fuller's influential feminist tract *Woman in the Nineteenth Century* published (revised from *The Dial*). Mexican−American War until 1848; Texas joins U.S.; other Mexican territory annexed at end of war.

1846 Religious revival in Amherst. Emily has already been expressing doubt to her more pious friend Abiah Root.

1847 Emily enters Mount Holyoke Female Seminary in September. Emerson's *Poems* published, given to Emily by Ben Newton in 1849. *Jane Eyre* by Charlotte Brontë (1816–55) published under pseudonym of Currer Bell.

1848 *August:* Emily withdrawn from Mount Holyoke by father. Emily Brontë's *Wuthering Heights* published. *December:* Emily Brontë dies. Seneca Falls Declaration marks beginning of American Women's Rights movement.

1849 Publication of *Kavanagh*, popular romance novel by poet Henry Wadsworth Longfellow; secretly given to Emily by her brother Austin.

1850 Another religious revival in Amherst; Edward Dickinson, Susan Gilbert and Lavinia Dickinson join First Church of Christ. Health of mother Emily Dickinson begins to decline. Publication of *The Scarlet Letter*, a 'romance' by Nathaniel Hawthorne (1804–64).

1851 Emily and Lavinia travel to Boston. Herman Melville (1819–91) publishes *Moby-Dick*.

1852 Edward Dickinson, conservative Whig Party candidate, elected to U.S. House of Representatives. Harriet Beecher Stowe's *Uncle Tom's Cabin* published in book form.

1853 Amherst–Belchertown railroad opens, promoted by Edward Dickinson.

1854 Family visits Washington. *Walden, or Life in the Woods* by Henry David Thoreau (1817–62) published.

1855 Emily and Lavinia visit Washington and Philadelphia. Edward Dickinson repurchases entire Homestead and returns family to paternal home; defeated in election in November; starts law partnership with son Austin. Mother Emily Dickinson begins to weaken; henceforth Emily and Lavinia run household, supported by domestics. Walt Whitman (1819–92) publishes *Leaves of Grass*. Charlotte Brontë dies.

1856 Austin joins First Church; marries Susan Gilbert (1830–1913), Emily's closest friend; Austin and Sue move into The Evergreens, built for them by Edward Dickinson next to The Homestead.

1857   Emerson lectures in Amherst, stays with Austin and Sue; Emily doesn't attend. Elizabeth Barrett Browning publishes her long narrative poem *Aurora Leigh*.

1858   Emily is writing poetry seriously, perhaps writes first 'Master' letter. Darwin publishes *The Origin of Species*.

1859   Emily meets Catherine Scott (later Anthon), a friend of Sue, and considers her a close friend until 1866.

1860   Edward Dickinson declines nomination for Lieutenant Governor of Massachusetts on conservative Constitutional Union ticket. Rev. Charles Wadsworth of Philadelphia visits Emily. Abraham Lincoln, of the antislavery Republican Party, founded 1854, elected President.

1861   *Springfield Republican*, respected Western Mass. newspaper edited by friend Samuel Bowles (1826–78), prints Emily's poem 'I taste a liquor never brewed –' retitled 'The May-Wine'. Friends begin to notice that Emily has been withdrawing gradually from society. Elizabeth Barrett Browning dies in Italy. Confederation of 11 Southern States secedes from the Union; *April*: Civil War begins.

1862   *Springfield Republican* 'Safe in their Alabaster Chambers –'. During 1862–3, a period of apparent crisis in her personal life, Emily writes about 300 poems. Frazar Stearns, son of the President of Amherst College, killed in action. *April*: Emily replies to article in literary magazine *Atlantic Monthly* by Thomas Wentworth Higginson, literary figure and former preacher, includes poems, asks if her poetry 'is alive'.

1863   *January 1*. Lincoln's Emancipation Proclamation frees the slaves.

1864   Two more poems by Emily printed; Emily in Boston seven months for treatment of eyes.

1865   By the end of this year Emily has written about a thousand poems. *April*: General Lee, Confederate Commander-in-Chief, surrenders; Lincoln assasinated.

1867   Austin supervises construction of new First Church

opposite Evergreens; Edward Dickinson gives dedicatory speech in 1868.

1870   Emily meets Higginson, who finds the visit exhausting. Family friend J.G. Holland becomes founding editor of important literary magazine *Scribner's*; although he has seen dozens of poems by Emily, he prints none.

1872   Edward Dickinson resigns Amherst Treasuryship, to be succeeded in 1873 by Austin. Publication of *Middlemarch* by George Eliot (1819–1880), completed.

1873   Edward Dickinson elected to Massachusetts House of Representatives as independent candidate.

1874   Edward Dickinson dies suddenly in Boston. Austin and Sue's third child and Emily's favourite, Gilbert, born.

1875   Mother Emily Dickinson henceforth bedridden with paralysis.

1876   Helen Hunt Jackson, Amherst-born poet and novelist who has become Emily's friend and correspondent, urges Emily to publish. George Sand, French woman novelist, dies (b. 1804).

1878   By now Emily has written over 1,400 poems. Some in Amherst think Jackson's pseudonymously published 'Saxe Holme' stories are by Emily; Emily's 'Success is counted sweetest', published anonymously in *A Masque of Poets* (No Name Series) after Jackson's urging, is thought by many to have been written by Emerson. Samuel Bowles dies.

1880   Judge Otis Lord, family friend and recent widower, visits frequently and discusses marriage with Emily.

1881   *July:* President Garfield shot, dies 19 September.

1882   *April:* Rev. Charles Wadsworth dies. *September:* Austin Dickinson and Mabel Loomis Todd begin love affair. *November:* mother Emily Dickinson dies after long illness.

1883   Nephew Gilbert Dickinson dies.

1884   *March:* Judge Lord dies. *June:* Emily has first attack of kidney disease.

1885   Helen Hunt Jackson dies.

1886   *15 May:* Emily Dickinson dies of kidney disease. First
selection of her poems published four years later in
1890, edited by Thomas Wentworth Higginson and
Mabel Loomis Todd. First *Collected Poems* published
1955, edited by Thomas H. Johnson.

INTRODUCTION

Split the Lark — and you'll find the Music —
Bulb after Bulb, in Silver rolled —
  ('Split the Lark — and you'll find the Music —')

Emily Dickinson (1830–86) was one of the indispensable poets in English; one of the very greatest English poets. Her accomplishment is so radically original that the entire model of what poetry can know (and write) changes when her work is taken into account. And when our sense of writing changes, our entire model of knowledge shifts. Emily Dickinson was a woman; she wrote consciously and with profound insight about her womanly life. If we who read her are women, her accomplishment enlarges our recognition of ourselves.

The poetry of Emily Dickinson was virtually unknown during her lifetime, although she wrote almost 1,800 poems and fragments. Since then, Dickinson has gradually gained acceptance as an important lyric poet, though her range has often been considered limited. Some of her more cheerful lyrics have been standard anthology poems in the United States for many years, thus inadvertently disguising her clarity and fierceness. A *Collected Poems* finally appeared in 1955,[1] and her rich and demanding letters were published in 1958.[2] Dickinson's poetry is now readily available in paperback, and specialist studies have begun to flood from the presses. One recent study begins by describing Dickinson as the finest American woman poet.[3]

Emily Dickinson was indeed American, and proudly so; she

was a middle-class New England woman, well educated in terms of the prevailing cultural norms. In 'The Robin's my Criterion for Tune −' she wrote that 'Because I see − New Englandly', even a queen in one of her poems 'discerns like me −/Provincially −'. There is some irony in the way Dickinson is using 'provincial' in that last line. Dickinson did not consider American literature to be provincial. Also, anyone who writes accurately must write from experience, from their own province. Dickinson's poetry is set in that immediate moment of existence, with little nostalgia for a more overtly poetic medieval past.

Dickinson's kind of excellence, her kind of womanliness and the kind of poet she was are all, however, much less self-evident. One function of Dickinson's accomplishment is to force us to reconsider what we understand by greatness, gender and poetic knowledge. By coming to know her, we come to know them in a different way. The terms 'poet' and 'poetry' may be the easiest place to begin.

In Dickinson's day, 'poet' was an unambiguous term; poets were those who wrote in verse, using regular metre and rhyme. There was some question of whether the free verse 'breath' lines of Walt Whitman's *Leaves of Grass* (1855) were 'poetry'. Dickinson developed her arguments through rich metaphors, slant rhymes, metrical variation, capitalization for emphasis, lack of titles, unconventional punctuation and highly condensed syntax. Most of her contemporaries assumed these innovations to be the result of ineptitude. The form of most of Dickinson's poems is simple: variations on the alternating four-stress and three-stress line of common metre. In quatrains rhymed a-b-a-b, this has for centuries been the traditional form of the ballad, the hymn and the children's rhyme. Common metre is a modest and flexible form, able to accept great stress without ever becoming slack. In the twentieth century a much greater complexity of poetic expression has prevailed, and acceptance of Dickinson's practice has advanced apace. Ironically, though, because she framed her experiments in common metre, Dickinson is now often read as expressing known themes, in an old-fashioned set form. Critical theories which agree to 'privilege' a small body of texts by treating them as 'literature' tend not to receive work readily if it comes from a new direction.

For the full force of Dickinson's expression to be seen her texts must be accepted as writing, not edged into the pantheon of the literary.[4] Exclusions from the literary are legion. The 'great poem' is usually an epic, a long poem or, failing that, a linked sequence of poems; writers of short poems like Dickinson are more readily considered minor. Many of Dickinson's most vivid expressions are found in her letters; when letters are not considered worth critical attention, her work is distorted. When the poet is a woman, her womanliness needs to be considered as a generative force in the poem, not as something that puts her in a sub-category of literature. Finally, when a poet's work has been neglected for as long as Dickinson's was, it can look peculiar because it has not had a clear influence on today's poetry. In this way the poet can be punished anew for having been punished in the past. When, as with Dickinson, her work informs and is informed by a female tradition, it looks mysterious as well, because the continuity of female tradition is unrecognized.

It is, in fact, easy not to know Emily Dickinson. Because she is such an original writer, she has tended to be described according to what she is not: not a man, not like Walt Whitman, not 'professional', not normal, and not married. A writer who is described as different from what we know is bound to seem difficult. A writer who is said to come from a group whose limitations we think we know — an old maid American Victorian recluse poet, for example — is going to look limited.

It is easy not to know Dickinson because the type she manifests — the great woman poet — is still in the root sense not known by our culture. And whenever there is ignorance, there are reasons why ignorance has settled in that particular spot. I also do not know Dickinson fully. Whenever I open her *Collected Poems* I find her describing some new state or arguing some new premise or pioneering some new use of language. I have also had to find my way out of assuming that because I am a woman I would know automatically what Dickinson would think, and accept instead the surprise of what she truly thinks.

Emily Dickinson has a lot to teach us, not least when she offers her awesomely accurate inside pictures of taboo subjects such as fear, hopeless longing, dread, death and loss.

For the non-academic reader, the many points where Dickinson diverges from literary tradition have little importance. Dickinson is a very direct writer, and the emotional tenor and major themes of her poems reveal themselves easily. Typically, she begins a poem with a powerful recognition:

> It was not Death, for I stood up,
> And all the Dead, lie down −
> It was not Night, for all the Bells
> Put out their Tongues, for Noon.

This imagery is complex and quick-changing, with a surreal image of church bells sticking out their tongues coming hard upon the eerie picture of the speaker as perhaps a vertical corpse. Yet the tone is unmistakeable − a nightmarish, fixed terror mixed with a curiously calm investigatory interest.

Even though her works have only gradually filtered through to a large public, there is a genuinely popular element to Dickinson. It is those trained in critical theory who find Dickinson 'different', because she doesn't fit a received model for literary greatness. I believe Dickinson's poetry changes literary theory. To think about how Dickinson wrote is to experience gaps and silences in the existing models. Reading her fully means redefining those models. It is an exhilarating sensation.

My discussion of Dickinson's poetry is broadly thematic rather than chronological. Because her poems weren't published during her lifetime, they remained in some senses aspects of mind, their processes and arguments available to her continued questioning. The fair copies of her poems which Dickinson bound into booklets or 'fascicles' from 1858 to 1864 (and left unbound thereafter) were returned to and revised over a period of years. Words were starred and alternatives written in at the bottom of the page. A number of revisions change the poems' themes and a few poems were revised heavily enough to become new poems. As Dickinson wrote over a period of about twenty-five years, her voice, her rhetoric, her music and, above all, her metaphors all became part of a rich repertory of knowledge. She could — and did — draw upon this repertory without explaining it further. Images that seem to be serving one kind of purpose in one poem appear in another poem with other facets of connotation emphasized. Since Dickinson wove her images economically, often in a single word, the word bears traces of its other uses.

In very general terms there is an 'early', relatively conventional Dickinson, consisting of her earliest surviving poems and continuing into 1859. There is a 'middle' Dickinson of passionately intense investigation, centring on her *annus mirabilis* of 1862–3 when she wrote about three hundred poems. In the late 1870s and early 1880s there are more poems of fixed, harsh irony, which might be said to mark out a 'late' Dickinson. 'Late' is, however, only a relative term; at the time of her death at the young age of 56, ageing was not yet one of Dickinson's topics. Such an arrangement doesn't work particularly well for Dickinson. One reason is the unchanging form: common metre remained her favourite form all her life. She also encourages a non-chronological reading by her practice of binding poems from different years together in the same booklet, and by not dating them. The numerous poems she sent in letters are only a limited help in dating, since while they obviously had been written by the date of posting, they could have been written much earlier, and often were.

Dickinson developed argument and figuration by turning to different facets of words and stances. I have adopted a kind of imitative structure for this book, exploring various facets of Dickinson's accomplishment as a means of circling inwards towards that never-quite-complete centre which is her 'difference'. Throughout, the effort is to use detail to indicate range. I want to convey at least a little of what Emily knew.

★

While I have tried always to choose the clearest word for the context, certain terms may not be immediately familiar to all readers. The following working glossary provides a kind of outline map of my concerns.

Dualism assumes a split between spirit and matter or mind and body; its greatest exponent was Descartes, but its premise of a split is at the core of Western philosophy. In the mid nineteenth century, philosophical **idealism** stressed the neo-Platonic ideal or higher aspect of the dualistic split. With its emphasis upon the metaphysical (that which is beyond the physical), idealism plays a large role in romantic thought and poetry. Its prime exponent in the United States was Ralph Waldo Emerson, the most influental cultural figure of Dickinson's day. **Transcendentalism** was the name given to the idealism of Emerson, Margaret Fuller, Orestes Brownson, Henry David Thoreau and others. Emerson and Whitman tried to set forth a **holistic view** of life, that is one in which all contradictions could be subsumed in a larger whole; this effort informs a tradition in American poetry, sometimes called the Orphic tradition, to which only a very few Dickinson poems belong.

Apart from its dictionary meaning **difference** (*différence*) has been taken by the French philosopher Jacques Derrida to mean a not-quite-definable disjunction, a sort of non-principled principle of discontinuity. **Epistemology** is that aspect of philosophy concerned with theory of knowledge and, by extension, theory of mind. **Heuristic** refers to a search for knowledge, a kind of investigative intellect which I find in Dickinson, though not in an abstract form. The philosophical and psychological **subject** is the person experiencing the emotion, as in the adjective subjective. When I discuss what a poem seems to be about, I use the term **topic**. The **object** is the other, the object of desire and fear. The primary object in all our lives is our mother.

So much Freudian terminology has entered everyday life that only a few terms need clarification: **manifest content** is that which is immediately visible; **latent content** is what is hidden beneath. **Sublimation** enables us to shift unacceptable drives into acceptable channels. Thus, according to Freud, is civilization formed. I have used **self** simply to mean the person, but the term has overtones of the separate, isolated ego. **Sex** is that biological difference which makes some of us women and others men. **Gender** is what a given society makes of that difference. I use femininity and the **feminine** to designate socially acceptable genderings of women; not all women are feminine. **Female**, meaning qualities arising from the female sex, is used to contrast with feminine. At times I have preferred to call Dickinson **womanly**, to stress the integration of thought, feeling and experience in her work. A complete body of work is the **canon**, whether the canon of English poetry, or the canon of Dickinson's work. Though a valuable term, it can be used to exclude as well as include.

Dickinson's poetry is rich in **imagery**, or sense impressions rendered in language. **Metaphor**, the representation of one object or quality by another, is a device (or **trope**) of substitution based upon resemblance. **Simile** is a comparison using 'like' or 'as'. **Symbols** are highly developed metaphors, often abstract, with deep cultural resonance, such as the cross, the rose, the colour purple. In the Western tradition, metaphor has tended to use the physical to help explain the metaphysical; with the loss of belief in the metaphysical, metaphor has come under attack, in both theory and practice. To avoid the assumption that they are always discussing symbolism, some critics now refer to the **signifier** (the metaphor word) and **signified** (what the signifier represents). The **emblem** is a particular kind of didactic metaphor, consisting of the detailed elaboration of meaning from a picture of a symbolic object. Essential to Protestant tradition, the emblem poem may be one of the bases for Dickinson's kind of metaphor. The **conceit** is an extravagantly unlikely metaphor, whose conceptual acrobatics give pleasure to the reader; it is characteristic of seventeenth-century Metaphysical poetry.

Despite her chosen distance from public discourse, Dickinson wrote **rhetorically** − that is, she used devices which are meant to argue and convince. Linguistic forms were for her so intimately part of knowledge that she often used terms such as syllable or syntax as metaphors for the physical.

Like many modern poets, Dickinson often uses **synechdoche**, or the representation of a whole by a part. She also uses **metonymy**, which is a non-symbolic substitution of one term for another. These terms are far from exclusive; perhaps the clearest indication of the presence of the metonymic is when neither term of the comparison is seen as more elevated than the other. Without pressing the case too far, one may discern parallels between psychological acts and linguistic devices; these are of particular importance for a poet like Dickinson, who concerns herself with representing inner states accurately. Thus the psychological act of displacement functions in the mind the way the metonym functions in language. In **condensation**, another essential mode of the unconscious, a single idea represents several chains of association. Because it is located at the inter-section of these associations, the condensed idea can have tre-mendous power; its linguistic equivalent is synechdoche.

'New' or invented metaphor usually takes effect by un-conscious connections, at the level of feelings.[5] One of Dickinson's main objectives is such a transfer of emotion; the more specific the signifier, the more precise the delineation of emotion.

These detailed descriptions of metaphor are necessary because much of Dickinson's unique use of it comes, in my view, from her treating it as if it were metonymy — that is, as if the signifier and signified were at the same level of figuration, and as if her substitution involved a shift of reference between two objects that have some relation *outside* language. At the same time, Dickinson takes great care to construct her own metaphoric diadem, or linked circle of connotation, *within* language.

CHAPTER ONE

DICKINSON AND KNOWLEDGE

Life, and Death, and Giants —
Such as These — are still —
Minor — Apparatus — Hopper of the Mill —
  ('Life, and Death, and Giants —')

Of Bliss the Codes are few —
  ('To her derided Home')

If Walt Whitman is the American poet of wholeness, Emily
Dickinson is the American poet of what is broken and absent.
She knows herself, but she knows by experience how the self
breaks upon its encounter with the way things are. Non-
mythological and anti-Platonic, Dickinson uses her art to break
open received certitudes. She is a heuristic poet, a poet of
investigation, of knowledge as value. Her poetry experiences
and argues and questions. Dickinson seems to have known
herself — that great assignment of Protestant tradition. Her
poetry assumes the presence of a feeling self, instead of
depicting a struggle towards self-knowledge. That knowledge,
however, is only the beginning of Dickinson's search for the
accurate representation of experience. She uses her nakedly
knowing self as a tool with which she can possess and
command abstractions such as time, space and death, and
emotions such as pleasure or pain. But by token of that same
close command, so-called abstractions in Dickinson are treated
as entities, qualities, things touched or touching.
  Dickinson addresses the abstraction as she experiences it:

> Pain — has an Element of Blank.
> It cannot recollect
> When it begun — or if there were
> A time when it was not —

Many Victorian poems describe unexamined abstractions, as if society agreed about what constituted sorrow or love. These could be personified, and their attributes could be listed and elaborated metaphorically. Dickinson takes on a frightening abstraction and evolves its attributes from experience, not tradition. In poetry and philosophy, the subject — the experiencing person — may wonder about the existence of other minds. Dickinson wrote many poems on this problem.[1] In 'Pain — has an element of blank', she contemplates the possibility that there may be circumstances in which the perceiving consciousness also does not exist, erased by its own emotion. 'The Soul has Bandaged moments —' she begins another poem; the abstract soul is a bandaged body, in a metaphor which denies dualism. Time is also represented physically, bound up by pain. As Dickinson concludes at the end of 'The Soul has Bandaged moments —', such recognitions 'are not brayed of Tongue —' in the public discourse of her society, or, for that matter, our society either.

Dickinson wrote about feeling, but out of feeling she constructed a theory of knowledge — not *beyond* feeling, or free from it, or in any way separate, but using it as a kind of knowing.[2] In effect — though not in conventional terms — she is an epistemological poet, a poet who advances a theory of knowledge. Dickinson made this concern explicit. After the forms of the verb 'to be', 'know' is the most frequently used verb in Dickinson's poetry, appearing 230 times, more even that any noun except 'day'.

Dickinson's constant pressure towards knowing means that she can treat even the most tormented situations with great calm. She can begin by writing 'I felt a Funeral, in my Brain', or 'Pain — has an Element of Blank —' or 'I felt my life with both my hands —' and then proceed to delineate that state with a commanding accuracy. In a manner more resembling the Metaphysical poets than her Victorian contemporaries, male or female, she uses emotionally heightened states as occasions for clarity.

American poetry characteristically embodies acts of process: the Dickinsonian 'process' is passionate investigation. Her investigative process often implies narrative by taking speaker and reader through a sequence of rapidly changing images, even when all the action is interior. These investigations structure Dickinson's poetry; I suspect that the flexibility of her investigative movement is the major reason why Dickinson generally was contented with common metre. She may even have enjoyed the way her condensed discoveries press against the limits of a small form.

Dickinson's poems typically begin with a declaration or definition in the first line and proceed to a metaphorical breaking open of the original premise. One poem will examine

> The Fact that Earth is Heaven
> Whether Heaven is Heaven or not.

Or she may declare: 'More than the Grave is closed to me —'. Or assert, and then question why, 'The Tint I cannot take — is best —'. Or she may address her discovery outwards: 'Tell all the Truth but tell it slant —'. Other poems, but fewer, begin with an observation, which forms the shell for the poem's argument: 'How the old Mountains drip with Sunset', or 'The Moon was but a Chin of Gold'. The middle of the Dickinson poem is usually a sequence of metaphors, or metaphoric actions. Then the poem veers, often unexpectedly, into surmise, renewed rhetorical inquiry, or an open closure. The dash that ends so many Dickinson poems is a graphic indication that the debate does not finish with the poem. While Dickinson's poems are short, they give a sense of enormous distances being covered, and of power forcefully directed to an end. Such poems do not need length; indeed, some are exhausted by the time they reach their close.

Dickinson's consistency does not come from a self or 'I', endlessly spinning out image and event from itself, as in the case of Whitman. Her consistency comes from the activity of her mind in poem after poem, constantly giving itself over to the question the poem is about. Dickinson assumes a continuously changing relation between herself as poetic subject and the object of her discourse. She may be present as a highly individualized 'I', only to use her situation to draw a psychological picture which is so accurate that the rest of us see ourselves in it; this is the case in the poem 'A loss of something ever felt I'. She may write as a more general lyric 'I', as in 'I think to Live — may be a Bliss', and then end the poem by veering towards a more individuated self. She may shrink her consciousness to that of a child or suppliant, often strategically, but sometimes out of apparent despair. Or she may dispense with the first person entirely, and write about he, she, it, they, or you; 'we' is a rare locution.

What Dickinson does *not* do with her speaker is equally important. She never uses the 'I' to presume an intimacy with an audience which is then meant to take her side, as Sylvia Plath can do. She doesn't rework her intimate history in public, as John Berryman and Robert Lowell do, to lay bare what went wrong. In fact it is notoriously difficult to extract actual events and people from Dickinson's poems. I mention these differences at this point, because Dickinson's investigations can seem to resemble the internalized, psychologized modern poetry of self. There has been a defiant return by so-called 'confessional' poets to the personal 'I' which modernism drove out, but where that self is self-important, or where that 'I' is pervaded by Romantic Promethean grandeur, it is again distant from Dickinson. Where there is a connection is in poetry by women which sees womanliness as a kind of instrumentality, as the shape through which a knowledge of feeling can come. As Adrienne Rich writes in the concluding lines of 'Planetarium':

I am an instrument in the shape
of a woman trying to translate pulsations
into images   for the relief of the body
and the reconstruction of the mind.

To paraphrase Whitman, Dickinson comes near to contradicting herself; she contains multitudes, but each facet of that multitude is accorded a separate poem. Thus the existence of a Dickinson poem on a given topic or state, such as the moment of death or the child's experience of loss, means that there are other poems exploring other possible assertions, facets, or questions thrown up by the topic, until 'topic' itself becomes an arbitrary term. Whenever I, or any other critic, may write that Dickinson does or does not assert something, chances are that there is another Dickinson poem which speculatively advances the opposite assertion. Dickinson's canon shows tendencies, it displays favoured, even obsessive, areas of investigation, but it offers few set themes.

The question of faith is one such topic for Dickinson. She wrote poems which assert belief in God and celebrate God's handiwork in Nature. She begins one poem:

> I know that He exists.
> Somewhere — in Silence —
> He has hid his rare life
> From our gross eyes.

Despite its blunt opening, however, this is a poem of desire and doubt. The delicate, disappearing God seems to be playing a game of celestial hide-and-seek. But what, the poem asks, would happen if the game should 'Prove piercing earnest —' and 'Death's — stiff — stare —' loom before the searcher? Then

> Would not the fun
> Look too expensive!
> Would not the jest —
> Have crawled too far!

It is only very generally true that Dickinson wrote about belief; she wrote about the experience of finding out about belief.

Dickinson's questioning poems can be said to be 'about' personal loss, the limits of sense, the body, love, time and eternity, or about the visible and the invisible, or about threshold states. More precisely, they are about the process of the mind seeking knowledge. It is this heuristic model, this investigative push, that constitutes the deep Dickinson theme.

Dickinson pursues that knowledge wherever it is to be found, no matter how it makes her feel. She reports her pursuit, seemingly as it occurs, with such profound attention that her poems offer exhilaration, no matter how sombre their topic.

To see Dickinson as an epistemological poet, a poet who advances a theory of knowledge in her work, doesn't mean that she is exclusively, or even primarily, an intellectual poet. She was brilliant, well educated, and confident in her use of conceptual, scientific, legal and linguistic terminology, but the truly remarkable quality of mind in her poetry comes from her refusal to separate this mind from the body and emotions which temper it. Dickinson writes close to the traditions of post-Romantic poetry and women's poetry in that her poetry expresses strong emotion. She stands to the side of it to the extent that the drive for knowledge dominates, and the affairs of the heart are seen as part of that knowledge, not separate. Hers is an epistemology of feeling. It is actually quite difficult to locate Dickinson's refusal to sublimate in literary-historical terms, because it is so alien to our usual structuring of dualism. Dickinson has the direct access to emotion which is thought to be — and is — a characteristic of much women's poetry. She doesn't, however, soften those emotions into acceptability or use poetry as an escape, either for herself or for her reader. Perhaps her knowledge has gone unrecognized for just this reason: she doesn't present it as a solution to human loss and pain. Rather, it is a way of experiencing fully and with utmost clarity whatever must be experienced.

Emily Dickinson's poetry runs the full emotive range from ecstatic celebration to numb despair. Huge shifts of perspective, imagery of thresholds, gems, open and closed space, stars, planets and firmaments mark Dickinson's sublime. In a few, very striking, poems she sees both human and writerly desire as capable of fulfilment. Imagery of plenitude — wine, feasting, nectar, flood and luxury — accompanies Dickinson's joyous knowledge. In these poems, her tone is often highly erotic:

Wild Nights — Wild Nights!
Were I with thee
Wild Nights should be
Our luxury!

As Dickinson would have known, the Latin word *luxus*, from which 'luxury' stems, means sensual excess or debauchery. Her declaration is actually redundant, further emphasizing its ecstatic triumph by the repetition of 'Wild Nights'. It is as if sensuous bliss is a state in which everything means the same thing, which is itself. The second stanza of 'Wild Nights — Wild Nights!' develops this oceanic emotion into a nautical metaphor as Dickinson, somewhat more conventionally, declares that 'Winds' are 'futile' 'To a Heart in port —'. Nor will this mariner need 'Compass' or 'Chart' to guide herself.

The poem's last stanza takes off from this hint of exultant freedom. The sexual beat of the rower's oars gives way to sheer exclamation:

Rowing in Eden —
Ah, the Sea!
Might I but moor — Tonight —
In Thee!

The last image may look like gender reversal, with the speaker seeing herself as the active partner, but Dickinson isn't concerned with whether or not her ecstasy fits Victorian convention. The image is one of choosing to be contained by the lover. Mooring tonight is a way of remaining eternally in the oceanic paradise of Eros.

Even so joyous a poem as 'Wild Nights — Wild Nights!' is phrased in the conditional mode: 'Were I with thee'. Many more Dickinson poems mix doubt about the speaker's social role with an arrogant mastery of art. Often doubt and power appear in startling proximity. In 'Perhaps I asked too large —', rather a light poem, Dickinson's autobiographical speaker remarks, in a matter-of-fact manner, 'I take — no less than skies —'. Dickinson doesn't seem to think that poetic range and expressive power pose any problems for her. Daily life, however, can pose serious problems of 'fit':

> My Basket holds — just — Firmaments —
> Those — dangle easy — on my arm,
> But smaller bundles — Cram.

Cosmic questions can fit easily into the 'basket' of the poem. Dickinson is playing with the image of herself, a woman with a basket of berries. The difference is that she sees this bucolic image from the inside, and the berries she has picked are worlds: 'For Earths, grow thick as/Berries, in my native town —'. Pettiness, however, can 'cram' the same space. The short last line and the harsh, physical 'cram' enforce the point.

'Perhaps I asked too large —' shows cosmic confidence, poetic command and personal doubt, while having nothing to say about fame or reputation. It also frankly uses imagery drawn from Dickinson's daily life as a woman, with no sense that this shouldn't mix with 'firmaments'. The poem isn't difficult, but it looks peculiar in a lyric tradition in which the poet's expressions of personal doubt are usually linked with fears about his creative power. Fame and love are interlinked, and the whole is to be expressed (even in this century) in consistently elevated diction and imagery. Thus in Sonnet XXIX, 'When in disgrace with fortune and men's eyes', Shakespeare asserts that he must 'alone beweep' his outcast state, 'Desiring this man's art, and that man's scope', until he remembers his beloved's love.

Dickinson's kind of knowledge made for 'difference' in both the usual and the philosophical sense of the term. Her difference from convention was recognized both by her and by her contemporaries. She knew she worked alone. 'Much madness is divinest Sense', she wrote in a famous poem, indicating that her divine sense might look like madness to others. The poem's conclusion is bitter: 'Demur — you're straightway dangerous —/And handled with a Chain —'. One of the bases for Dickinson's difference was her inexorable recognition of the incomplete: 'difference' in the philosophical sense. For her there is no complete ideology. Like the theoretician Jacques

Derrida a century later, Dickinson uses a kind of working hypothesis of 'difference', some never quite definable root principle (or anti-principle) of the discontinuous which, if accepted, makes all immediate fragments, gaps and illogicalities the normal state of things. Derrida actually spells his term 'différance', so as to emphasize its distinction from its consequences in everyday 'difference'. Dickinson, writing amid the metaphysics of the mid nineteenth century, was resolute in her aesthetic of difference, but she felt the pain of loss of complete presence in the world. Derrida, long after metaphysics had been discredited by linguistic philosophy, raises the same issue of comfortingly complete 'presence' and dismisses it confidently.

Dickinson and a modern philosopher have been temporarily bracketed here for a reason. Mind—body dualism has dominated Western philosophy since Descartes. Most post-Romantic poetry has some aesthetic of the broken. Mario Praz called the early break-up of personality into irony 'romantic agony'. T.S. Eliot discerned a 'dissociation of sensibility' between intellect and feeling beginning much earlier, in the mid seventeenth century. Dickinson too is broken, but the rift she perceives occurs along unusual lines. The woman, her feelings, her intellect and her writings are usually whole in Dickinson; the anguish — the rift — comes from her balked encounter with others, with time, with unknowing, and with death. Because she is honest, Dickinson admits the inner hurt that comes from this 'difference'.

Mid nineteenth-century European writers (and some American writers) began to consider the divided self, usually working along lines of conscious and unconscious. At the same time, Emerson turned to formulations of wholeness, a line which Whitman followed. Dickinson recognizes the American holistic consciousness, but she recognizes it as a fiction. In her poem 'I think to Live — may be a Bliss' she declares that wholeness is 'Beyond my limit to conceive/My lip — to testify —'. Her *pro forma* declaration of inadequacy turns into its opposite as she proceeds to conceive of blissfully complete presence in brilliant imagery. The passage has a significant literal import, however.

Her lips are never going to testify in public about life; she is a woman who writes rather than speaks. It would be lovely, Dickinson writes, if her heart could be as vast as the sea, and she could feel

> No numb alarm — lest Difference come —
> No Goblin — on the Bloom —
> No start in Apprehension's Ear,
> No Bankruptcy — no Doom —
>
> But Certainties of Sun —
> Midsummer — in the Mind —

In such a state of earthly completion, she would not feel dread about any kind of difference, whether it would be change in time, or fear, or loss. Dickinson spends a stanza vividly describing negative apprehensions. Then she suddenly rescues the power of the blissful vision with 'Certainties of Sun', her image of the moment of the mind's apogees; this 'Midsummer — in the Mind —' anticipates 'Credences of Summer', Wallace Stevens's long poem of earthly bliss, written over eighty years later.

The mind's pleasure in contemplating wholeness is so intense that it becomes a kind of mirage of bliss:

> The Vision — pondered long —
> So plausible becomes
> That I esteem the fiction — real —
> The Real — fictitious seems —

But Dickinson is a poet of the real, of the way things are to mind and body. Only 'the way things are' is genuinely knowable; in a curious way this frankness is evidence of Dickinson's nearness to the American pragmatic tradition. To know feelings precisely is one mode of accuracy. Ezra Pound was probably edging in the same direction fifty years later when he wrote 'A Few Don'ts by an Imagist', a set of instructions which served as a kind of negative manifesto for modernism. One of the rules of the new poetry, Pound declared, should be 'Direct treatment of the thing, whether subjective or objective'. Direct treatment of the subjective 'thing' was, at least theoretically, a goal of the new movement.

The vision of 'plenty' in Dickinson's 'I think to Live −' is a fiction, a sense picture of something desired. The desire, not the vision's lovely content, is the way things are. Dickinson concludes the poem with a swerve sideways on the link of desire; all this fiction would be true if her life until now had been a 'Mistake/Just rectified − in Thee'. The poem ends there, without clarifying whether 'Thee' is God, or a person, or both, or another fiction. 'Thee' is whatever would give the mind whatever the mind desires.

Knowing desire, and knowing lack, absence and loss, are not small areas, as Dickinson well knew. A good part of her particular wisdom lies in her poetry's acceptance of loss and lack as being available to knowledge. To know loss is still to know. Sometimes that knowledge serves to destroy every impulse towards fiction. In 'Finding is the first Act' Dickinson unravels the myth of quest, using the tale of Jason and the Golden Fleece as a narrative basis for her own negative parable:

> Finding is the first Act
> The second, loss,
>
> Third, Expedition for
> The 'Golden Fleece'

The impulse to go on quests has its origin, Dickinson suggests, in previous loss. So the hero's accomplishment may simply consist of finding something to substitute for what he has already lost: in Freudian terms, to sublimate for infantile finding and loss of the mother. If this is the case, whether or not the quest is successful, it is a fraud; those who go on quests are being fleeced.

Bit by bit, as it adds up the narrative elements, the poem subtracts everything, even the epic hero:

> Fourth, no Discovery −
> Fifth, no Crew −

> Finally, no Golden Fleece —
> Jason — sham — too.

Dickinson is deconstructing the idea of myth-making.

There is a hint here of a quality that marks the poetry of Dickinson's twentieth-century post-Protestant successor Elizabeth Bishop: narrative requires a confidence, a sense of being at home with the world that the poet herself does not have. Bishop looks out at landscape more than Dickinson, but both poets leave story-telling to others. A mistrust of fiction, particularly Greek mythology, is central to the radical Protestant tradition which informs American literature. As late as 1837, in *Twice-Told Tales*, Nathaniel Hawthorne wryly puritanized Greek mythology for the New England sensibility. In an important late poem, 'The Bible is an antique Volume —', Dickinson writes that she prefers pagan song to a Bible dictated 'by Holy Spectres'. While she deconstructs Greek myth in 'Finding is the first Act', she attacks Biblical narrative here. She remarks that 'Orpheus' sermon captivated —' through poetic melody, while the harsh condemnatory tones of the Bible make it sound like a hack novel with 'Eden — the ancient Homestead —/Satan — the Brigadier —'. Greek mythology isn't the enemy; what Dickinson is rejecting is the goal-oriented optimism of the narrative, particularly quest narrative.

Most of Dickinson's lyrics do in fact have a narrative element. After the Ah! of pure lyric emotion, all poems tell a story. The tale of the Dickinson poem is the line taken by the poem's perceptions, as if her mind were a film camera cutting abruptly from one scene to another, sometimes superimposing images through her compact metaphors. Her mental narratives have the flavour of fantasy, nightmare, science fiction, the gothic, and the nineteenth-century sensation novels she enjoyed reading along with Shakespeare. At times the movement of her poems also resembles types of religious vision such as Thomas à Kempis's *The Imitation of Christ*, a book she knew well. In their cosmic range, some even resemble the narrative of The Book of Job or the visions of Revelations.

The difference seems to be that she doesn't give her inner narrative a mythic authority in itself.

In the many poems in which Dickinson does not formulate even a fiction of bliss, she faces the reality of loss. It is one of her most important recognitions. As Dickinson explores loss, she finds it has a specific shape for the emotions. It occurs arbitrarily, without reason. In her letters as well as her poems, she shows no ability to insulate herself or deflect the shock of withdrawn affection, departure or death. Every time it hurts as if it were the first time. After the event, the mind, ever seeking causality, may busily construct reasons why the hurt should have happened. Perhaps God decided it would happen – then, that way, to that victim. One of the most important differences between Dickinson and her Puritan forebears is that she does not accept the concept of original sin. For her, it is perverse for us to have to suffer as we do. Also, for Dickinson, loss is not made good through later rewards in heaven for those who suffer on earth. The Christian economy of rewards for the just and punishment for the wicked has ceased to function for her. Loss simply happens. Yet the state of loss itself can be understood, and the act of coming to understand it is the act of a mind shaping itself.

Dickinson's poem 'A loss of something ever felt I –' examines childhood loss. The 'I' of the poem accommodates itself to autobiographical reading. Dickinson (though not her friends, father or brother) saw her childhood as one of repression and deprivation. The 'I' of the poem is sad, not through mere mood, but in mourning for love withdrawn when she was too young to articulate what had been lost:

> The first that I could recollect
> Bereft I was – of what I knew not
> Too young that any should suspect
>
> A Mourner walked among the children

The brevity of the sketch universalizes the state it describes. To be conscious is to be conscious of loss; the two states are experientially indissoluble. 'A loss of something ever felt I' ends with the image of the adult mind, like a prince cast out

of his rightful 'Dominion', 'softly searching', perversely but
fruitfully, in the opposite direction from the traditional objects
of Christian quest:

> I find myself still softly searching
> For my Delinquent Palaces —
>
> And a Suspicion, like a Finger
> Touches my Forehead now and then
> That I am looking oppositely
> For the site of the Kingdom of Heaven

'A loss of something ever felt I' neither gains heaven nor
assuages the speaker for its loss. With a critical glance at
Wordsworth's imagery of childhood bliss, it analyses the state
of the child and then the adult looking, hopelessly, for the
infantile heaven of undifferentiated, unseparated, unconscious
existence. The goal of the poem is to know and depict what is
in fact a classic human state of loss — even if this knowledge
contradicts received Victorian truths about childhood.

Just what is the Dickinson poem 'about'? Who is it about?
What event is it relating? What is the symbolic meaning of this
or that word? Only rarely does Dickinson allow a definite
answer to such questions, and many critics have found her
ambiguity troubling. I have just sketched some ways of understanding what Dickinson's poems concern themselves with, but
this does not do away with the habit of wanting a clear meaning
and researched references. The problem arises from us, from
our received habits of reading — it isn't Dickinson's problem.
Not knowing a reference in Dickinson's writing doesn't block a
tonal reading of her poems. Indeed, I suspect that her poems
open themselves to direct reading *because* of this supposed
'problem' of ambiguous references, not in spite of it. She is
directing her energy where she wants it, to the issue, state
or question she is investigating. The interpretative habit of
translating the literary text into something else turns Dickinson's practice into a problem. Dickinson's poetry can be
difficult or irritating to interpret in psychoanalytic or New-
critical terms, since both methods assume a distinction between

surface or manifest content and meaning or latent content. Dickinson's poetry can be deconstructed and, as I have said, a case can be made for seeing her at least partly as a poetic deconstructionist, but it resists translation.

In the past, and still for some people today, Dickinson's ambiguous references have been seen mainly as a challenge to the biographical interpreter. The great effort has been to attach poems to purported relationships in Emily Dickinson's life. In Dickinson's poem 'My life closed twice before its close —' the 'twice' has been taken to represent the end of Emily's love relationships with her teacher Benjamin Newton and the Rev. Charles Wadsworth.[4] Another reading has proposed Kate Scott and a second, unknown person.[5] Or it may be the death of Dickinson's parents, or other people's deaths, or a love and a death — since Dickinson's editor couldn't date the poem, no event can be excluded. These efforts are unedifying, and not merely because the guesses could be incorrect. The poem is not a lament. It states how things are. Then it asks whether heaven is going to unveil a 'third event' comparable to the earthly loss which has already been, 'So huge, so hopeless to conceive'. The parallelism implies that heaven can only parallel the structure of earthly loss. Immediately after this comparison, the poem ends its questioning with two of Dickinson's most famous lines:

> Parting is all we know of heaven,
> And all we need of hell.

Heaven and hell manifest themselves through the same effect: in practical terms — and these are the only terms the poem is considering — they are both hellish.

The wish to find the 'secret' meaning of a poem in its personal address can affect any poem, particularly poems written in the first person. This tendency is the literary—critical version of gossip. However, some gossips are more harmful than others. A cultural bias already determines the way we read writing by women. Women's writing is traditionally thought to be merely personal, merely a cry of the woman's circumstance. One consequence is that interpreting works according to events in the life of the author is especially damaging to women writers. To the extent that a poem may be seen to be merely 'about' how awful it is that a man has lost interest in the writer, it ceases to have interest for anyone else. Unless, of course, it is interesting as a means of reinforcing what our culture already thinks about female psychology.

Dickinson didn't make her references ambiguous in order to pose problems for later critics, even though, like most people until recently, she certainly wished to keep her private life private. Whatever their presumably multiple purposes might have been once, the present function of the unclear or absent referent is to keep attention on the process of gaining emotional knowledge which these poems definitely *are* about. If Dickinson was indeed writing occasional poems about specific people and events, then she coded her autobiographical allusions very carefully. No one has been able to say for sure who Emily's mysterious lover was, whether there was more than one, or if she loved not a man but a woman. Although some of her poems are reactions to specific events, few such events have been traced, the major exceptions being elegies and poems relating to the Civil War.

Dickinson confounds the literal-minded searcher by sending the exultant poem 'Title divine — is mine!' to Samuel Bowles, sometime in 1862. Since the next line declares that the speaker is 'The Wife — without the Sign!' the case would seem clear. When one notes that the same poem was sent to her close friend and sister-in-law Sue Dickinson, everything — including Emily Dickinson's sexual orientation — is suddenly less clear. Just how literal is 'Wife' meant to be? Similarly, the intimate 'Going to Him! Happy letter!' which says that there is another 'page I didn't write', is usually considered to have been sent to Bowles (although there is no surviving evidence). However, the poem exists in a second version, with different pronouns: 'Going — to — Her!/Happy — Letter!' Very likely Emily Dickinson was in love with both Bowles and Sue. Very likely too that she generalized from her experiences, distorting, condensing and displacing them as she restructured them. The biography is raw material. It is interesting to know whom a poet loved, if we can find out reliably, but it is a sinister interest if it shrinks the poem down to the size of its signified — its referent.

Nevertheless, the effort to pin down references in Dickinson can have some benefits. Dickinson sent hundreds of her poems to friends, family and literary correspondents. Comparing the inner, familiar address of a poem to the way it addresses us, its later, outer readers, can tell us a great deal about Dickinson's voice. The actual or potential doubled address gives many Dickinson poems a kind of impersonal intimacy — the quality I have been describing in other contexts as 'frank' or 'direct'. Also, Dickinson was a highly allusive writer, packing connotations into the small basket of her poems. When she quotes or paraphrases Shakespeare, the Bible, standard recent authors, her female contemporaries or a recent article, she always works at an angle. She is always offering a comment, often ironic, on the material. The more of these allusions we know, the closer we come to being able to define Dickinson's irony.

In Dickinson's powerful short poem 'We play at Paste —' it is the symbolic referent or signified that is teasingly ambiguous. By not fixing what the metaphoric language of the poem refers to, Dickinson creates an absence. It is an absence of the signified, that usually abstract or metaphysical quality which the poem's metaphors have been representing. Once we recognise absence, our attention is thrown back even more sharply at what is present. In the first half of the poem,

> We play at Paste —
> Till qualified, for Pearl —
> Then, drop the Paste —
> And deem ourself a fool —

Paste, Pearl and the nature of the qualification aren't defined. As a consequence, the poem's stress falls on the narrative, which shows how we learn our craft on false or cheap models (represented by the metaphor of 'paste' or imitation gems) until we are qualified to work on the real thing.

Although it would go against the poem's silences to do so, it is possible to speculate about references. The poem can be packed full with presence. Perhaps in 'We play at Paste —' Dickinson might have written — unusually for her — a theologically optimistic poem. Perhaps in a loose, Emerson-like mingling of Platonic and Eastern notions of the Beyond, she sees earthly life as an illusion and earthly action as mere practice for the perfection of eternity. Or we can opt for a different set of references, and find that 'We play at Paste —' may be describing the lessons to be learned from misplaced youthful affection. Once we have found the true Pearl or beloved, we 'deem ourself a fool', — love's fool. The poem's metaphors could also apply with perhaps greater acuity to the poet's passage from apprenticeship to the practice of poetic truth.[6]

The second stanza of 'We play at Paste —' looks at the issue from the other side, once achievement has been reached:

> The Shapes — though — were similar —
> And our new Hands
> Learned *Gem*-Tactics
> Practicing *Sands* —

Dickinson had studied geology; she knew that grains of sand and diamonds are both crystalline, and she used this knowledge to give precision to her theme. In 'Auguries of Innocence' William Blake had written similarly:

> To see a World in a Grain of Sand
> And a Heaven in a Wild Flower

Where Blake stresses the presence of the infinite even in the smallest, Dickinson writes about how we can pass from one state to the other, meanwhile finding that the new materials have the same structure as the old. Her poem is about process, his is about vision.

The question of symbolic reference also connects with the ways Dickinson's poems develop their sign systems. The definite, blunt, almost monosyllabic quality of Dickinson's figurative language ('Paste', 'Pearl', 'fool', 'Tactics') can lead the reader to assume an equivalent bluntness of reference, a reference both metonymic and obvious. In 'We play at

Paste —', Dickinson is using these simple words in a manner which parallels the poem's act of process. In effect she is writing that words which designate material objects or acts have the connotative resilience to suggest other actions. These other actions may be different or more elevated, but our relation to them is structured the same: we engage ourselves in playful work with them. Tactics are tactics. The process of moving upward serves to call attention to links.

This pointing at specific words marks all of Dickinson's poems, whatever question they address. Such a continuity would seem to argue that she doesn't have one type of figurative language for 'personal' poems and another for 'philosophical' ones. More effort spent evolving symbolic meanings would not necessarily produce results. Sometimes in Dickinson there is a rune or riddle to be cracked, but the meaning lies inside the word or through links between words, not beyond them.

The same images enter other poems with different emphases. The pearl reappears in the poem 'Your riches — taught me — Poverty', in which a 'Pearl' 'slipped my simple fingers through —/While just a Girl at School'. Here, the facet of the pearl which means love of knowledge seems to be stressed, while the spiritual connotations of the 'pearl of great price' of faith (Matthew, 13:46) or the 'one pearl' which makes up the gate of the heavenly city (Revelations 21:21) are less evident. Dickinson used the words 'pearl' and 'pearls' thirty times in her poems; each use plays on the others until all facets of her 'pearl' have been displayed.

Dickinson's model for her cross-referenced image clusters was almost certainly Shakespeare. The condensed figurative language of the tragedies seems to have come particularly close to her desired use.[7] She weaves words from *Antony and Cleopatra* and *Hamlet* into her poems and letters particularly often. When it is said of Coriolanus that 'he painted with shunless destiny', (*Coriolanus* 2, ii) the line sounds eerily like Dickinson, even down to the coining of a negative by adding the suffix '-less'. For Shakespeare, however, the frame of reference for figurative language was the play, while for Dickinson it was her entire post-1858 output, faceted and reflected through individual poems. As a result, Dickinson's poetry repays long-term re-reading; metaphors which seem opaque at first take on radiance when refracted through other poems.

The pearl and diamond of 'We play at Paste —' are part of a large image cluster of jewels and gems which Dickinson used as the basis for her theory of metaphor. In 1852 she wrote that she had had 'feelings so like gems' (*Letters*, I, p. 181). She called Chapter 21 of Revelations the 'gem chapter' (*Letters*, II, p. 601). In an important letter to her literary friend Joseph Lyman, she wrote, paraphrasing *Hamlet*:

We used to think Joseph, when I was an unsifted girl and you so scholarly that words were cheap & weak. Now I dont know of anything so mighty. There are [those] to which I lift my hat when I see them sitting princelike among their peers on the page. Sometimes I write one, and look at his outlines till he glows as no sapphire.

(Sewall, II, p. 675)

The gem-like important word stands graphically separate in the Dickinson poem, capitalized and set off in space by dashes, like a jewel in a bezel. Dickinson is, if anything, over-specific in her word choice, preferring the singular to the plural, the gem-like emblem to lists of examples. There is a kind of object display of individual words in her work. This trait is most evident in her use of geographical place-names as metonyms. In 'Volcanoes be in Sicily' she is 'Vesuvius at Home'. In 'Ah, Teneriffe!' she addresses a specific mountain range instead of the mountain as type of retreating presence. When Dickinson links images of gems with those of crowns and diadems, she is thematizing her characteristic process of connecting gem-words with other words in a ring. In the passionate poem '*One Life* of so much Consequence!' Dickinson represents herself as a pearl diver, ready to die for one pearl:

The Sea is full — I know it!
That — does not blur *my Gem*!
It burns — distinct from all the row —
Intact — in Diadem!

The pearl and diadem refer with equal ease to love and writing, or rather love and writing are both kinds of crowns. In several poems she crowns herself or is crowned, both as lover and poet. 'I choose, just a crown', she remarks at the end of 'I'm ceded — I've stopped being Theirs —'.

The crown merges with the image of circumference, another key term. Dickinson sees herself not as a poet of the holistic centre, but of circumference. This was not necessarily a small assignment. As she wrote in July 1862, in her fourth letter to Higginson: 'Perhaps you smile at me. I could not stop for that — My Business is Circumference'. (*Letters*, II, p. 413). When circumference is at its smallest, as in the poem 'A Coffin — is a small Domain', the grave is a 'Circumference without Relief'. At its most vast, it leads Dickinson into unusual vagueness, as when she addresses 'Circumference thou Bride of Awe'. Usually it offers a way of expressing power, particularly the linguistic power to contain meaning. One advantage of the circumference metaphor is that it allows for absence, for space, without being destroyed. Circumference is the assignment Dickinson gave herself, but she carries out her business by linking the gems of distinct, individual words. In terms of figurative language, this is a metonymic impulse, substituting rather than transcending, finding the meaning inside or next to the signifier. Dickinson's revelatory gems are not very distant from the stones of William Carlos Williams's 'a Sort of a Song' in which, in an etymological pun, Williams declares that 'saxifrage is my flower/that splits the rocks'.

Dickinson's linked words do not deny the desire to transcend.[8] Perhaps the best way to describe the relation between the metaphysical and language in Dickinson is to say that she could desire the infinite, but that she chooses to express even that desire in a figurative system of container and contained. This is potentially a dangerous procedure; where a link is absent, the word's glitter may prove opaque. In Dickinson's practice, however, each facet or gem constantly refracts meaning at a slant back to another word. Each word can be seen to have the magic power of all its link words, while still remaining 'intact'.

CHAPTER TWO

DICKINSON AND DIFFERENCE

Over the fence —
Strawberries — grow —
Over the fence —
I could climb — if I tried, I know —
Berries are nice!

But — if I stained my Apron —
God would certainly scold!
Oh, dear, — I guess if He were a Boy —
He'd — climb — if He could!
  ('Over the fence —')

Captivity is Consciousness —
So's Liberty.
  ('No Rack can torture me —')

Heavenly Hurt, it gives us —
We can find no scar,
But internal difference,
Where the Meanings, are —
  'There's a certain Slant of light')

My approach to Emily Dickinson's poetry is necessarily feminist. Dickinson's womanliness is at the heart of her accomplishment, and critical awareness of gender is essential in understanding not only her themes, but also her poetics of difference.

Emily Dickinson was a poet who had a theory of knowledge. Her epistemology, her view of the shape of knowledge, included the perspectives of her female sex and the social gendering of women. Her poems and letters constantly address specifically female problems of identity, fulfilment and freedom in relation to the conventions of the time. In fact, Dickinson analysed the conditions of female life with such reckless frankness that her darker perceptions are still frightening to our therapeutic age.

Much present feminist scholarship has turned away from acknowledged literary masterpieces and from the concept and study of genius, recognizing these as terms whose values have served to validate the cultural establishment which proposed them in the first place.[1] Until these values can be sufficiently reassessed, 'women's writing' may be a more productive area for feminist scholarship, teaching and reading than, say, 'women and literature' or 'images of women in fiction'. The idea of women's writing permits us to examine the literary market-place which determines the women's writing that aimed at publication. The idea of a distinct female tradition means that the reader is free to find value in private or 'amateur' writing, and to find other connections between writers besides those of great men and their followers. From this perspective, 'writing' and 'literature' are merely descriptive terms, not expressions of relative value. The immediate consequence of this enlargement of frame is that more writing becomes available to knowledge and pleasure.

It is at this point that the feminist project and at least part of the deconstructionist project converge;[2] both question the privileging of the consciously literary great book, preferring the undetermined 'text'. Both find value in intertextual play. Dickinson's style of literary feminism diverges from deconstruction when it comes to the role of the text. While she plays with linked chains of signification in her intertextual metaphors, her play is in deadly earnest: Truth is the one abstraction that Dickinson doesn't mock. The truthful poem — truthful perhaps because it admits discontinuities and doesn't insist upon 'presence' — is immensely vital to the person. And deconstruction does not consider the person, only the texts.

Emily Dickinson plays a double role for feminist theory.

First, as a woman who wrote highly original poetry without denying her womanhood, Dickinson is a major definer of any womanly line in English poetry. She herself saw a distinct female literary practice in mid-nineteenth-century writing, and located herself in this literary sisterhood. For the moment, however, I wish to look at the second aspect of Dickinson's importance for feminist reading. Dickinson is a poet of such power and originality that her example directly engages the poetic institution. If women's poetry has seemed to be one thing without Dickinson's accomplishment, then its terms change when she is added. If American poetry has seemed to centre around a Romantic idea of self as developed through the holistic poetics of Emerson and Whitman, then Dickinson shifts that centre towards a poetic of knowing which is rhetorical, doubting and emotionally direct while its figurative language is highly coded and complex. The shape of poetry in English changes when Dickinson is admitted. She made the lyric a kind of poetry that can ask anything. Her rhetoric argues and declares itself in complex, highly elliptical syntactic structures of a sort not usually found in lyric. Such an increase in range is particularly striking in the nineteenth century, when the field available to poetry was thought by most poets and critics to be shrinking.

But merely to add Dickinson's poetry to the existing canon would be to have it remain an anomaly, even a curiosity. The goal is to show how the canon itself can be changed. Every period has its own canon, which is that body of poetry that seems to make its own theory, whether of life or of language. A work is part of the canon if it seems important to the arbiters of culture of any given period. The canon is what we read when we want to think of our literary tradition. Since the received canon can function as a kind of living definition of what the language can say at its most intense and artful, it has tremendous potential for creativity. Since it reflects dominant ideology, the canon can also be used to peripheralize writing which has not hitherto been seen to be part of it. The canon can change dramatically; in this century the most striking instance has been T. S. Eliot's reintroduction of the

Metaphysical poets and his attack upon the Romantics; change can also occur slowly, as the role of writing as a whole is seen to change. The present-day canon does not yet admit women to the centre, but Dickinson changes this by moving the centre towards women.

When Dickinson's accomplishment is fully appreciated, past poetry — male and female — is likely to look different from the way it looks now. Out of this fresh model of the past — a past we haven't, so to speak, arrived at yet — we may develop a new poetics for our future use. I am stressing the future of the past because Dickinson's impact has yet to be felt. Because she wasn't published, Dickinson played only a minute role in the development of writing in her day. She did influence her friend Helen Hunt Jackson, a best-selling novelist and poet, but that was because Jackson saw Dickinson's manuscripts, met her and corresponded with her.

The fact that Dickinson's poems weren't published is virtually the first thing one hears about her. Of the 1,774 poems and fragments, only ten were published during her lifetime. These were given titles by the editor, and they were editorially altered. As was often the custom in newspaper publication of the day, they appeared anonymously. There is reason to think that Dickinson selected poems on recognizably conventional topics when she sent them for publication, though even this ploy didn't always succeed. Some of her best poems were rejected, even when, like the poem 'At Half past Three, a single Bird' they were 'about' such approved feminine subject matter as birds. Most of the published poems are amongst the group that has subsequently made up the anthologized Dickinson: 'Success is counted sweetest', 'Some keep the Sabbath going to Church —', and 'A narrow Fellow in the Grass'.

After 'A narrow Fellow in the Grass' had been published as 'The Snake' with its third and fourth lines jammed together, Dickinson wrote to her literary 'preceptor' Higginson that the poem was robbed of me − defeated too of the third line by the punctuation. The third and fourth were one − I had told you I did not print − I feared you might think me ostensible.

   (*Letters*, II, p. 450)

Silence looms as a necessity for self-respect.

   The history of Dickinson's publication has also been a history of the dispute over who should possess Emily. Family, social class, gender and region all made reductive claims, denying her 'difference' to keep her in their control. After Emily's death in 1886, her younger sister Lavinia found her manuscripts and realized the extent of her literary production. After a false start with Susan Gilbert Dickinson, the sister-in-law who had once been Emily's closest friend, Lavinia took Emily's booklets and scraps to Sue's enemy, Mabel Loomis Todd, a young woman of literary aspirations who had since the early 1880s been having a well-known affair with Sue's husband Austin Dickinson, Emily and Lavinia's older brother. The posthumous 1890 *Poems* by Emily Dickinson, edited by Mabel Loomis Todd and Thomas Wentworth Higginson (by then a respected literary elder statesman), contained 115 poems. It was a critical and financial success, going through eleven editions in two years, and Todd and Higginson brought out a second culling, *Poems*, Second Series, in 1891; a third (edited by Todd alone) appeared in 1896, with Todd's selections from Dickinson's letters coming in between in 1894. Todd and Higginson freely altered Dickinson's poems, adding titles, regularizing rhymes, changing punctuation and capitalization, and sometimes substituting their own metaphors for Dickinson's. Higginson began to wonder just how Dickinson's actual topics could be defined, and he noticed ways in which her startling illuminations resembled those of Blake. Nonetheless he and Todd organized their editions by abstract thematic categories which the poems were meant to be 'about'.

   As a general principle, whenever the cultural assessment of a writer corresponds to that society's received image of the way someone of that sex, class, race or nation would behave, we have reason to be suspicious. Dickinson entered the twentieth century seeming to have written the over-sensitive, coy, rather ill-disciplined poems one would expect from a well-bred New England spinster of legendary eccentricity. Dickinson herself knew that women were supposed to be ill-educated and dependent, and she deliberately reinforced this cliché at least once while first seeking professional criticism of her poetry from Higginson.[3] Nor did family circumstance help. Since Dickinson's papers were divided amongst warring family members, self-serving gossip flourished in print, especially on the subject of this or that thwarted love affair.

Even in a national literary history which has been marked by massive revaluations, Emily Dickinson's 'case' is still astonishing. A hundred years after her death, her work is undergoing tremendous shifts in its perceived significance. One reason, as we are seeing, is painfully simple: it was literally not possible to read Dickinson's poetry in full until thirty years ago. After Todd and Higginson's editions, Dickinson family members added more poems and letters bit by bit in 1929, 1932, 1935 and 1945, and there were two perceptive studies of Dickinson in the 1930s.[4] Only in 1955 did a complete Dickinson appear, edited by Thomas H. Johnson, with the poems in the form that Dickinson wrote them. All the Dickinson letters then available were published in 1958, edited by Johnson and Theodora Ward. Jay Leyda's contextual collection *The Days and Hours of Emily Dickinson* came out in 1960, and Richard B. Sewall's magisterial biography was published in 1974.

Literally as well as figuratively, Emily Dickinson has only truly come to light in the last ten to fifteen years. She did not greatly influence the development of modern poetry. Poets and critics such as Allen Tate, Conrad Aitken, Theodore Roethke and (most significantly) Sylvia Plath read Dickinson, but always as a partial case: as fascinating or surprisingly good, considering what she was. Probably the most perceptive modernist reading of Dickinson is to be found at a greater distance, in the intense, sombre, rather surreal translations of her work by the German poet Paul Celan. Many critics now accept Dickinson as one of the major English poets, but there is still a tendency to pin undesirable qualities on her, as prophetess of a fragmentary, introverted or neurotic voice. By contrast, in feminist criticism, Dickinson's voice has become one of the ancestral voices informing the language of the womanly, for speech in life as well as in poetry.

The ways in which the suppression and distortion of Dickinson's poetry differ from the misunderstanding of, say, Herman Melville's novels and poetry can provide a useful working measure of the role played by gender assumptions in the reception of literature. While such a comparison would yield valuable information, it is not a major objective of this study. For my purposes it is more useful to consider how Dickinson's public silence and private, written eloquence generated and then guarded what seems to have been a chosen 'difference'.

It was Whitman who wrote, at the end of 'Song of Myself', that after he died he would meld together with the American earth so that 'If you want me again look for me under your boot-soles'. Whitman knew well that his poetry was not likely to be understood. He also seems to have reckoned that there was no single authorized meaning for poetry, even if the poet may have had a specific intent. Instead, there are many kinds of poetic absorption, all cleansing and healthy.

> You will hardly know who I am or what I mean,
> But I shall be good health to you nevertheless,
> And filter and fibre your blood.

'You', however, will always be there. There will be a posterity. Whitman's only question is where that posterity will catch up with him:

> Failing to fetch me at first keep encouraged,
> Missing me one place search another,
> I stop somewhere waiting for you.

Dickinson gave up such hopes of a posterity. That hopelessness is essential to her truth-telling. It cleanses her address. It also gives us the assignment of formulating the moment when we have arrived at the point − or points − where Dickinson has stopped.

In her poem 'This is my letter to the World', Dickinson famously described her poetry as a 'letter to the World/That never wrote to Me'. Perhaps because it displays elements of the self-pity that one would expect from a poet who presumably feels left out, 'This is my letter' is a popular poem. The message, which seems to come in this instance directly from Nature, 'is committed/To Hands I cannot see – '. While Dickinson wrote some poems about fame, succcess and publication, she didn't comfort herself with the vision of a more understanding future audience. Rather, she used its absence.

When Dickinson chose her 'difference' above a compromised success, she became a free writer. Whether or not anyone was ever going to read, let alone understand, her investigations, she carried them out on her own, in writing, for about twenty-five years. This was a decision of great courage and, equally, great stamina. Which of us could claim the strength to do the same? Dickinson suffered deeply from the lack of love and loving discourse with equals, but as a poet she preferred her own knowledge to the 'balm' of the social discourse available to her. She went her way alone.

> My secret as secure
> As Herschel's private interest
> Or Mercury's affair –

In this poem, 'Nature and God – I neither knew', Dickinson is remarking that her knowledge is about as secret and un-important as the most important astronomical discoveries about the universe. It is as safe and firm, that is, as Herschel's discovery of the planet Neptune. The planet has been there all the time, so Herschel's knowledge, once gained, can't be undone. It is a knowledge about as 'private' as the shape of the solar system or the amorous business of the messenger-god Mercury (also a planet, lest her discovery seem too purely mythic).

Dickinson wrote several poems about how, and why, she removed herself from the economy of literature. In the most famous she wrote angrily:

Publication — is the Auction
Of the Mind of Man —
Poverty — be justifying
For so foul a thing

Dickinson is saying two things at once in this stanza, as she often does. Poverty is used as the justification for sale of self in the literary market-place, but those who sell themselves to the highest bidder only grow poor. Using the emotionally charged image of a slave auction, Dickinson indicates that these sellers enslave their own minds.

After revealing the consequences of selling one's self, Dickinson goes back a step to attack the original terms according to which publication is defined:

Possibly — but We — would rather
From Our Garret go
White — Unto the White Creator —
Than invest — Our Snow —

Her royal 'we' would rather go straight from the impoverished poet's garret to God; the alternative, if one admits it is possible, is a kind of logical joke, a category mistake: to publish poetry is like trying to invest snow. Snow melts; perhaps Dickinson is saying modestly that since her poems are ephemeral, it would be inappropriate to invest them. But a classic Dickinson irony based on connotative links makes such modesty suspect. 'We' and the snow-poem and the Creator are all white. White writes white: her poem is God-like. With the same image Dickinson has also taken into account the chance that unpublished poetry may, like an untarnished God, have something chilly about it. To be born white and go straight to God is not to have lived.

Women's poetry is 'different' because we know it is by women. The social definition of gender role reaches inside the poem. As a woman writer, Dickinson partakes of this larger difference as much as any of her sisters. This is the case despite her considerable cultural advantages. Emily Dickinson was a white woman, born into the New England professional élite.

She never needed to work to survive. Even her use of poems as gifts is entirely in keeping with the exchange of manuscripts among genteel friends of an earlier era.[5] Most importantly for her, she was given the opportunity to develop her mind. She had an inspiring education at the co-educational Amherst Academy and then went on to attend Mount Holyoke Female Seminary (later College) for a year. She studied the arts (English literature, rhetoric, 'mental philosophy', Latin, French, German, history, geography, classics and Bible study). Also, unusually, she had an excellent grounding in the sciences (mathematics, geology with the famous Professor Edward Hitchcock who lectured at Amherst, botany, natural history, physiology and astronomy). All these show up in her poems. Emily Dickinson's formal education went far beyond anything available to any British woman writer until almost the turn of the century (and then to very few). Dickinson's intellectual self-confidence contrasts tellingly with Virginia Woolf's life-long perceived inferiority and anger at having been excluded from cultural institutions because of her sex. In her letters Woolf notes bitterly and repeatedly how she had to educate herself in her father's library, while young men of the same background went to Eton and Cambridge as a matter of course. Woolf's *Three Guineas* (1938) is a tirade against self-important male instutitions such as Cambridge, which in the late 1930s did not even grant women full degrees.

Nonetheless, despite her education, Dickinson is not read as an 'educated nineteenth-century person'. It is her female sex which is the central determinant. The sex of a writer cannot be dismissed as background or excluded from 'objective' inter-pretation. Although poems are ostensibly read purely as literary works (as least when one reads a poet for the first time), in fact we almost always know the sex of the author. Since virtually all names are gendered, we can recognize that a poem is by a woman or man at the same moment that we learn of possible national origin, and usually before we become aware of class, race or literary allegiance. Emily, Marianne, Elizabeth, Muriel, Gwendolyn and Sylvia are all women's names, so when we read Dickinson, Moore, Bishop, Rukeyser,

Brooks or Plath, we know what we are reading. Hilda is female too, so Ezra Pound changed Hilda Doolittle's name to the neutered modernity of 'H. D. Imagiste'.

Our knowledge of the writer's sex has a profound effect upon our reading. The effect is all the more powerful because formal or academic or materialist reading is not meant to recognize sexual difference. Yet since critical readers are men or women, they naturally recognize it instantly. In the absence of an accepted way of understanding relations between gender and form, that recognition remains unconscious, inarticulate and, as a result, not subject to criticism. Those qualities which can be perceived as not those of the dominant ideology can be attributed to the group of which the writer is seen to be a member, so that the poem's 'difference', instead of seeming a contribution, appears to make it merely typical — typical (in this case) of the sex of the author.

Work by members of the dominant cultural group is, ironically, readily perceived to express difference, but those differences are credited as expanding or redirecting the expressive range of a literary genre. John Berryman can be credited for reinvigorating the sonnet form, for returning syntactic experiment to the lyric (if one hasn't noticed it already in Dickinson), and for developing a childlike persona as a means of exploring the unconscious; he doesn't tend to be described as writing typical heterosexual white man's poetry. The dominant norm is of course a myth: every member of a privileged group can point to something he or she does not have or know and see himself as not responsible. Virginia Woolf, for example, was greatly angered at criticisms of 'Bloomsbury' in the late 1930s by the young Desmond McCarthy and Ben Nicolson; sensitive to sexual discrimination, she turned a blind eye to the advantages of her class. And the myths of difference change, like the canon of accepted literary works which forms one of their cultural supports. When Simone de Beauvoir wrote in *The Second Sex* that women are the sexual 'other', that-which-is-not-male, she seemed to hold out hope that women of intellect, particularly in France where the intellectual is a privileged category, might escape from otherness and be accepted. Later, de Beauvoir realized that at the moment when she was finally being complimented (with interesting frankness) for being able to think like a man, she was also being told she was not a real woman, since women can't think.

The social and psychological purpose of defining difference as 'other', as aberration from the norm, is to maintain that norm. It has, however, the consequence of causing over-reaction to difference. Difference is fearful. It vitiates the strength of the norm through its presumed strangeness; because it has been kept down, its power is always seen to come from below. Freud's early hydraulic model of psychic economy, with consciousness on top and the subconscious beneath, is also, unsurprisingly, a model of social economy as well. Just as in white racism, one drop of black blood makes its bearer black, as in writing, when we know the work is by a woman, one drop of what can be perceived as feminine or womanly makes the work part of a sub-category of women's writing – or simply less good. If, on the other hand, a man writes work with 'feminine' qualities of sensitivity and direct emotion, it is not necessarily seen as feminine, since the masculine gendering of the norm, being unarticulated, isn't recognized as a norm.

At this point it may be objected that what is being described is a masculine problem. So it is. It is also a problem for women. We live in a male society, and society models thought. The habit of seeing difference as aberration is infectious. Also, men don't have a monopoly on prejudice. In her essay collection *Sister Outsider*, the American poet Audre Lord has written with some irony about her position as a middle-aged black lesbian feminist socialist in a society in which each of these categories is presumed to dictate some predictable behaviour or form of expression. Lord has sought to redefine and rescue 'difference'. Racism, sexism, heterosexism, homophobia:

The above forms of human blindness stem from the same root – an inability to recognize the notion of difference as a dynamic human force, one which is enriching rather than threatening to the defined self, when there are shared goals.[6]

Female poetics is the as-yet-undefined sexual writerly 'difference'. Do we define that poetics from the outside or the inside? The female poetics may be the result of the woman writer's self-perceived difference from the culturally central, implicitly masculine model of self, self-consciousness and appropriate style. The woman writer then engages in a continuous revision of herself from object of discourse to speaking (or, more often, writing) subject. Socially, however, she remains the woman-object, that body which is 'other', which is looked at and is the object of desire. In this formulation, if a woman writer fails to write in a manner that her society perceives as feminine at that point, she can lose her position in society. This happened to Kate Chopin when her 'immoral' novel *The Awakening* was published in 1899. Chopin was a widow bringing up several children in the stratified society of St Louis. She solved the problem by ceasing to write. Tillie Olsen's *Silences* records many more instances in which 'difference' (of sex, class, race) was turned into silence.

Equally, in the feminine formulation, not being feminine can also destroy the inner position from which the woman writes, since she is always by definition writing 'as a woman', in the way her society defines women. Her literary self must carry out its investigations inside the frame of the culturally imposed gender model. She must not know anything a lady would not know. If she knows too much, her voice disappears, and she finds herself writing as no one, or as one of her society's negative images of women: the witch, the lesbian, the ravening beast, the monster, or the unsexed 'thing'.

Emily Dickinson was highly sensitive to her difference, not only from a masculine model, but also from the received model for feminine writing. She took up the challenge of identity and wrote as no one: 'I'm nobody! Who are you?' She also frequently writes as a witch, a feline beast (tiger and leopard), a monster, a 'thing' or a woman who loves women.

Heterodox voices are routinely excluded from whatever rewards culture has to offer:

> Civilization – spurns – the Leopard!
> Was the Leopard – bold?

Deserts — never rebuked her Satin —
Ethiop — her Gold —

This sensuous female feline can't change her spots. Nor does
she want to. 'She was Conscious', Dickinson tells us, so as to
avoid placing her leopard persona in the position of being
unconscious nature to male culture or 'civilization'. Wittily
correcting the assumptions of a patriarchal 'Signor', Dickinson
remarks that it 'was the Leopard's nature' to be spotted and
'Tawny', that is, flecked and imperfect but by the same token
ruddy with life — perhaps like the freckled, auburn-haired
Emily Dickinson.

Memories — of Palm —
Cannot be stifled — with Narcotic —
Nor suppressed — with Balm —

This Leopard does not have the option of sleeping her heritage away; she can't deny 'her Asia', her sensuous inheritance
of 'difference'.

Dickinson can simultaneously express the pathos of the
excluded and the commanding irony of one who knows herself
superior:

Why — do they shut Me out of Heaven?
Did I sing — too loud?
But — I can say a little 'Minor'
Timid as a Bird!

In 'Why — do they shut Me out of Heaven?' Dickinson offers
to temper her song for the purposes of getting into a heaven
whose conditions of entry have been set by others. If, she
remarks later in the poem, *she* had been Peter, the 'Gentleman'
in the 'White Robe', she would have freely given entry to all
who knocked at heaven's gate. But she isn't Peter, and she
knows it. Her only practical option is to make herself small,
and 'Timid as a Bird', like the sentimental women poets of the
period. Perhaps then she'll be let in through the door of
subjection that society keeps open.

It is possible, though difficult, to stand up and defend one's complex identity; in her bold poems Dickinson seems to say that she is what she is, whatever label others may put on her. It is much harder to defend oneself if one does not know the cause of the rejection. Always, for the writer, or person, who is 'different' there is the terror that one has been rejected because of something unforgivable, but unknown, that one has done. Since the punishment is silence and the closed door, the miscreant can never learn for certain which, if any, of her actions constitutes the crime.

Often, as we have seen, Dickinson takes a strong line on her identity, rejecting society's terms of judgement as well as the actual judgement, and boldly accepting the exclusions of difference. In another poem, she declares she would not live 'A Plated Life — diversified': switching to the conditional, her mode of hope and fear, she continues, '— 'tis when/A value struggle — it exist —'. In many other poems, however, she examines other facets of imposed difference as denial. Often this recognition of denial is associated with debilitating fear that no action she takes will ever go unpunished. In these poems Dickinson is bravely exploring what is in fact the classic root situation of masochism. Those who are constantly punished are being trained for self-operating punishments: if I am unloved, it is because I am unlovable. Whatever is done to me, I deserve it. Dickinson's poems illuminate the steps by which this dark path is prepared for the 'different'.

In 'Why make it doubt — it hurts it so —', Dickinson writes that her sexually neuter loving creature, the 'it' of the poem's first line, could be brave unto death for its love if need be. It might even enjoy dying for the sake of its beloved. What it cannot endure is unknowing. While it is 'So strong — to know', being forced to 'guess' makes it 'sick'. It begs its 'Master', the patriarchal beloved, not to deny it knowledge, even if that knowledge will only inform it of the conditions of loss:

> But — the Instead — the Pinching fear
> That Something — it did do — or dare —
> Offend the Vision — and it flee —

And They no more remember me —
Nor ever turn to tell me why —
Oh, Master, This is Misery —

There is something frightening about Dickinson's accuracy in assessing the bitter consequences of 'difference'. Women (and men, for that matter) tend to be afraid to admit the emotion that Dickinson depicts in 'Why make it doubt — it hurts it so —', because masochistic longing is one of those emotions which our society considers 'typically feminine'. Until the fear of admitting the hurt has been met with knowledge of what hurts, and why, we deny our ability to know ourselves. The importance of this knowledge is being recognized. As Adrienne Rich has remarked in *Of Woman Born*,

I believe increasingly that only the willingness to share private and sometimes painful experience can enable women to create a collective description of the world which will be truly ours.[7]

Rich is writing about falsifications of motherhood; in 'Why make it doubt — It hurts it so' Dickinson is giving the inside view of an annihilating dependency. Yet Rich's emphatic question *'But what was it like for women?'* is one which Dickinson answers.

In fact, Dickinson is depicting a half-way house on the road to masochism rather than masochism itself. The poem offers a clear reason why the creature has had the silent treatment inflicted on it. It — the creature — has 'dared' something, very likely said or written something, since the punishment which fits the crime is to have 'it' erased from the consciousness of the master race. Much of the speaker's pain comes from the punishment far exceeding any putative crime. Presumably Dickinson made her creature an 'it' rather than a 'her' to defeminize and generalize the state (although the poem later moves back into 'me'). She is trying to locate the characteristic experience of mystifying loss.

Dickinson's effort to address the case and not the person is particularly significant in this poem, since much of its imagery is very close to the draft of her third 'Master' letter:

Low at the knee that bore her once into ~~royal~~ wordless rest ~~now~~ Daisy
~~stoops a~~ kneels a culprit − tell her her ~~offence~~ fault − Master − if it is
~~not so~~ small eno' to cancel with her life, ~~Daisy~~ she is satisfied − but
punish ~~do not~~ dont banish her − shut her in prison, Sir − only pledge
forgive − sometime − before the grave, and Daisy will not mind −
      (*Letters*, II p. 391)

In this abject and tormented letter to an unknown male
recipient (perhaps Samuel Bowles), it is Emily who will never
know her fault. The knowledge revealed in 'Why make it
doubt' reaches into theological speculation. Dickinson hints
that the Master for whom her creature would die like a faithful
dog may not actually be a person but an idea, a 'Vision', which
the creature itself may have invented. In that case it has
invented its own torturer. Or 'They' who impose the sadism of
silence upon her are God or gods which, once challenged,
withdraw, like the 'Melancholy, long, withdrawing roar' of
the Sea of Faith in Matthew Arnold's 'Dover Beach'. If so, this
absence can annihilate the creature, since it fears that it itself
may have only existed as a figment of the visionary consciousness. No matter who has invented the fiction of Master and
slave, it is a fiction that kills.

'Pinching fear' is a state our culture attributes to women.
No matter how carefully or specifically a woman depicts it, no
matter how much she emphasizes the general case, she does so
at the risk of being thought typically feminine. It can be just as
difficult − and much less praised − to grasp the nettle of the
so-called feminine as it is to appropriate so-called masculine
qualities. There have been many great chroniclers of feminine
loss, both in the nineteenth century and this. I have noticed
that readers tend to find one of these writers to be revelatory
and incisive, while displacing 'bad' feminine traits of self-pity,
excess emotion, etc., onto the others. Thus one may admire
Dickinson, but find fault with H.D., Jean Rhys, Elizabeth
Smart, Sylvia Plath, Kate Millett (as novelist) or Anita
Brookner. (With Rhys, there is a case for direct influence: her
novel title, *Good Morning, Midnight*, is a Dickinson first line.)
From a feminist perspective one can also miss the contributions

of gay writers such as David Plante, who have taken up issues of fear and loss by getting outside the frame of the socially gendered masculine. Some writers do, of course, wallow in their own emotions. It is worth noting, however, that the writers listed above are all notable stylists. Perhaps style commands what the heart cannot.

CHAPTER THREE

THE HOUSE OF THE FATHER

— My Mother does not care for thought — and Father, too busy with his Briefs — to notice what we do — He buys me many Books — but begs me not to read them — because he fears they joggle the Mind. They are religious — except me — and address an Eclipse, every morning — whom they call their 'Father'.

  (Emily Dickinson's second letter to Thomas Wentworth
  Higginson, 25 April 1862, *Letters*, II, p. 404)

Emily Dickinson analysed and rejected much of what she was offered by her culture. She also felt rejected herself, even though she lived all her life in the house of her father. Literal and figurative versions of that father and that house play a large role in her thought.

  Emily Dickinson had no literary 'foremothers'. Her mother, Emily Norcross Dickinson, played a background role. Although she was a good cook and housekeeper, and a woman of tender feelings, she 'frowned with a smile' (*Letters*, III, p. 929) and she seems never to have understood the intellectual curiosity of any of her children. Nor did Emily feel nurtured by her. 'I never had a mother', Emily said to Thomas Wentworth Higginson when he visited her in 1870. She qualified her shocking remark only slightly: 'I suppose a mother is one to whom you hurry when you are troubled' (*Letters*, II, p. 475). Emily Norcross Dickinson became most important to her daughter during her long years of invalidism after a stroke in 1875, when she became the child and her daughter nurtured her. As Emily wrote to her close friend and 'sister' Mrs Holland,

We were never intimate Mother and Children while she was our Mother — but Mines in the same Ground meet by tunneling and when she became our Child, the Affection came —

(*Letters*, III, pp. 754–5)

Or again, shortly after her mother's death in 1882, Emily wrote to Judge Otis P. Lord that 'I cannot conjecture a form of space without her timid face' (*Letters*, III, p. 753). Although her mother had in some way failed her, Emily wrote in the poem 'To the bright east she flies' that her death had left the survivors 'Homeless at home'.

What Emily Dickinson did have was a powerful father, who represented the law in his community as well as in his household. The figures of father, 'master' and symbolic father cast a long shadow on Emily's emotional life and religious belief — and they influence (but don't determine) her idea of literary tradition as well. The life of Edward Dickinson sheds light upon Emily Dickinson's relation to the American Puritan inheritance, since Emily accepted some of her father's conservative values while attacking and denying others. By looking closely at Edward Dickinson we may see the shape of Emily Dickinson's loving resistance, a resistance which contrasts significantly with that of other literary daughters such as Elizabeth Barrett [Browning], Margaret Fuller, Virginia Stephen [Woolf] and Sylvia Plath, or Dickinson's American contemporary, the feminist leader Elizabeth Cady [Stanton].

Edward Dickinson of Amherst (1803–74) was an eminent public man, a lawyer, orator, and pillar of the community who is now remembered for his failure to understand his daughter. He would not have appreciated this historical irony. At the time of his graduation from Yale University in 1823, Edward Dickinson struck his friends as a bright and spirited young man, but he hardened early, in both public and private life. He had a sober courtship of Emily Norcross from nearby Monson, Mass., in which he declared his goal to be 'rational happiness' (Sewall, I, p. 47) and business success. In 1826 he married and set up a legal practice in Amherst. Edward Dickinson had patriotic and progressive views about women's potential: 'If they had opportunities equal to their talents, they would not be inferior to our own sex in improving the sciences' (Sewall, I, p. 49). He acted on these principles, offering his daughters an education equal to that which he gave his son. He seems, however, to have reneged on Emily, pulling her out of her university education at Mount Holyoke after a year (though the enforced religiosity of the institution may have made departure a relief). Also, unfortunately for his poet daughter, Edward Dickinson held classic nineteenth-century views about the innately masculine and the innately feminine. Creative women were well and good, but their 'difference' made them innately unsuited to the proper duties of womanhood:

I should be sorry to see another Mme. de Staël — especially if any one wished to make a partner of her for life. Different qualities are more desirable in a female who enters into domestic relations — and you have already had my opinions on that subject —

(Sewall, I, p. 49)

This was a letter to his fiancée Emily Norcross; these forcefully reiterated opinions may well have been the basis of the future Mrs Dickinson's all-too-successful self-effacement. As Sewall remarks, it was just as well that Edward Dickinson was too busy with his briefs to notice what his dutiful daughter was getting up to.

Although Edward Dickinson was a precise contemporary of Ralph Waldo Emerson (1803–82), his ideas were never altered by an encounter with Romanticism, and his political stance was one of literal conservatism — conserving the Union (of the United States) without subjecting any of its institutions to moral scrutiny. Always, the law came first. A life like Edward Dickinson's marks, in many ways, the dead end of Puritan tradition. In him, the marmoreal exterior and patriarchal belief in the rule of law are no longer complemented by a complex and questioning Puritan conscience, or a faith that history was God's re-enactment of the life of a chosen people in a new land. His daughter noticed this absence. Some of this empty form shows up in her imagery; the figure of the father, the Master, or God the Father is never accorded an inner self. The father never doubts or is divided. The 'house' of such a father may become a sepulchre, as Dickinson shows in the inexorable imagery of 'Safe in their Alabaster Chambers −'. This house contains a preserved ideological corpse. It is dead, but intact.

Once, memorably, Edward Dickinson rang the Amherst church bells to bring the townspeople out to see a great display of the aurora borealis or northern lights, but the exuberance, sensitivity to Nature, sincerity, and personal warmth which the next New England generation valued so highly were beyond him. When Edward Dickinson died in 1874 and Samuel Bowles, editor of the *Springfield Republican*, wrote his obituary, Bowles could apply what were by then Emersonian truisms and declare that Dickinson had not 'understood himself'.

It is important, however, to recall that Edward Dickinson was not considered peculiar for a man of his generation. When George S. Merriam, the biographer of Samuel Bowles, described the ideological background of western Massachusetts, he found in it values which were also those of Edward Dickinson. It is worth quoting Merriam's description at some length, since it expresses the struggle of mid and late nineteenth-century Americans to define their distance from the Puritan heritage. Merriam is condescending, but he is also in awe of the values which were then believed to have created the American republic. Also, significantly for the reader of Emily Dickinson, what Merriam is describing is not seventeenth-century Puritanism, but its survivals in the era of the Republic. Merriam leaves out the guilt and repression which informs Nathaniel Hawthorne's critique of Puritanism in *The Scarlet Letter* and *The House of the Seven Gables*.

Appropriately gendering the spirit of New England as male, Merriam wrote that it 'roused men with the ideal of a great destiny':

The ideal of conduct which it offered was austere but lofty. It appealed to the sense of obligation rather than to sympathy or delight. It made men strong rather than sweet; it made them sober, chaste, and upright. From whatever source derived, – from Puritanism, from the older Christianity, from English stock, from Hebrew religion, from primitive humanity, – the sense of duty lay deep in the New England character. Conscience was the bed-rock of the typical New-Englander, as granite as the foundation of his soil. Deficient in spiritual imagination, severely logical in intellect, he was in the practical conduct of life the loyal servant of Duty.[1]

Edward Dickinson spent his life as a servant of duty. Treasurer of Amherst College for 37 years from 1835, and the first citizen of Amherst, he was elected to the Massachusetts State Senate in the 1840s. He reached the peak of his career when in 1852, standing on the conservative Whig ticket, he was elected to the U.S. House of Representatives. (At the time the Whigs opposed the Jacksonian Democrats, who favoured widening the electoral franchise and making greater wealth available to the populace.) He attended the Whig National Convention of 1852, which supported both the Missouri Compromise of 1850, extending slavery into the new territories of the West, and the notorious Fugitive Slave Law, which ruled that an escaped slave could be pursued and recaptured anywhere in the United States.[2] In 1860 Edward Dickinson's name was canvassed as candidate for Governor of Massachusetts. During the Civil War (1861–65) he was an ardent supporter of the Union cause, though he had no commitment to the anti-slavery movement. Returned to the state legislature in 1872, he died at work in Boston two years later.

Edward Dickinson's politics were those of stasis. When the great Whig orator Daniel Webster came out against the anti-slavery movement, he pulled the Whigs with him. The Whig convention of September 1851 declared that it would 'respect the duties imposed by the constitution' (Merriam, I, p. 93), terms which, in the political code of the day, meant respect for the legal right (considered to be constitutional) of southern slave owners to have their fugitive slaves returned. When Dickinson stood for Congress he did so, as Bowles's biographer put it in 1885, as a representative of a party bankrupt in principles save devotion to the Union. He was one of the old 'river Gods' of the Connecticut River Valley, a politically and theologically backward-looking area of western Massachusetts. The 'Patriarchal Institution', as slavery was known, elicited no moral response from him. His proposed candidature in 1860 was on behalf of a rump, constitutionalist wing of the former Whig coalition.

In Edward Dickinson, there is a moral vacuum inside the edifice of law. In him, as in his daughter's poetry, law is the law of the father; its existence is predicated upon power rather than upon justice or equity. Her father's oppositions may also be reflected in certain indifferences in Emily Dickinson. As Shira Wolosky has shown, she was well aware of the Civil War.[3] The death in battle of young Frazar Stearns, the son of the President of Amherst College, shocked her deeply. Imagery of slavery and freedom, of union and secession, of struggle and imprisonment, runs through many of her poems of the period. She did not, however, comment upon the freeing of the slaves when Lincoln's Emancipation Proclamation took effect on 1 January 1863, and in general the sufferings of black Americans seem to have taken place at a mental as well as a physical distance from her (though she did read Harriet Beecher Stowe's *Uncle Tom's Cabin*).

Perhaps the shape of Edward Dickinson's life can best be represented by the symbol both he and his daughter used, namely the Dickinson Homestead. The Homestead is still one of the most imposing residences in the college town of Amherst, Massachusetts. A handsome, substantial, two-storey brick building with windows set symmetrically on either side of a Federal-style classical portico, it was built in 1814 by Emily Dickinson's grandfather, Samuel Fowler Dickinson, a man much respected locally for his work in establishing Amherst College. Held by local tradition to have been the town's first brick residential house, it is the home of people who do not suffer material want. The Homestead stands on a bank behind a hedge, which was low in Emily's day, but is now grown up into trees. Its front door is several steps up above the paved walk, which is itself somewhat elevated above Main Street. In the nineteenth-century Main Street was, appropriately, a main road into Amherst from the east and Boston.

Edward Dickinson locked his family and himself into The Homestead. He grew up there and lived there after his marriage. It must have been a profound shock to him when his father, whose physical (and mental) health and finances were failing, suddenly sold a half interest in The Homestead in 1833 and moved with Edward's younger siblings out west to Ohio, never to return. Edward and his young family stayed on, uncomfortably sharing The Homestead with its new half-owner, until in 1840 they sold out and moved to nearby North Pleasant Street (everything was nearby in the small town of Amherst). In a westward-facing nation, Edward Dickinson's ambition was to stay in his home town, to win back the Homestead his father had lost, and to keep his children in that home. His triumphant repurchase of the entire Homestead in 1855 held tremendous import for Edward and his by then grown children. By returning to his nest, he had in no uncertain terms become his own father's father, erasing family shame in the most positive material fashion.

Once resettled in his Homestead, Edward Dickinson kept his children near him, but he gave them little intimacy or warmth, either before or after 1855. 'I always ran Home to Awe when a child' (*Letters*, II, p. 517), Emily Dickinson once wrote. This awe felt to her like her only nurture: 'He was an awful Mother, but I liked him better than none.' Her beautiful elegiac comment sums up this chilling love: 'His Heart was pure and terrible and I think no other like it exists' (*Letters*, II, p. 528). Possibly Emily Dickinson's happiest homage to the spirit of her father was her love for Judge Otis P. Lord, a man of her father's generation and politics, who had known the Dickinsons for many years. After Judge Lord was widowed in 1877, he called on Emily and, on the evidence of her loving and playful letters, he seems to have asked her to marry him. At this time, Sue Dickinson unkindly claimed to have seen Emily 'in the arms of a man' at the 'immoral' Homestead (Sewall, I, p. 232). Very likely she had seen an embrace between them. Emily enjoyed her late happiness, even if she did not feel she could move from Amherst to Salem and run the household of a public man.

Neither of Edward Dickinson's daughters married, which was unusual in a well-to-do and well-connected family. While he naturally said nothing that has survived on the subject, Edward seems to have selected Emily to stay with him, rather the way Emerson chose his clever daughter Ellen Tucker Emerson to be his lifelong companion after it became clear that he and his wife had ceased to communicate. Ellen Tucker Emerson travelled with her father, while Emily's role was to be at home.[4] The giveaway of abnormality here is not the extraordinary Emily. She was able to turn personal fate into a vehicle for vocation, redefining her entrapment as freedom from the social obligations of wife and mother, and using her disdain for mediocre company to give her privacy to work. She drew a sharp distinction in 'Title divine – is mine!' between the spiritual bride, who is 'Betrothed – without the swoon/God sends us Women', and the actuality of contemporary wifedom after what she called the 'soft Eclipse' of marriage. The surprise was Vinnie, the ordinary daughter, who impressed all as someone made to be married, but who somehow never did marry. From our perspective, Vinnie's historic role was to give Emily the basis for the second family she constructed herself, the family of sisters (see Chapter 8).

Austin Dickinson, Emily's sensitive and intelligent older brother, hardly got further away from The Homestead. After a brief stint at law school and teaching in Boston, he returned to Amherst, where he joined his father's law firm. Austin and his bride Sue Gilbert were settled next door in The Evergreens, built for them by Edward. In 1874 Austin inherited his father's job as Treasurer of Amherst College, and he played a comparable social role to his father's in Amherst, supervising the building of a new First Church opposite The Evergreens, and laying out the improved town common and the new cemetery. Austin's ambitions stopped at the edge of town. His marriage to Sue, vigorously promoted by Emily, was visibly unhappy – an instance perhaps of Emily's passionate affections hurting other people besides herself.

Today The Homestead is partly a museum and library of Dickinsoniana. Owned by the Trustees of Amherst College, it is open to the public on certain days by appointment. Inside The Homestead, one flight up on the left, western, side of the building, is the corner bedroom where Emily Dickinson slept in a single Empire-style bed and wrote her poetry and letters from her twenty-fifth year until her death in 1886. A bright, light, medium-sized room, it has two windows looking south across Main Street to what was once a field owned by the Dickinsons. When Dickinson spoke of herself as going from her 'garret', in 'Publication — is the Auction', she was writing both figuratively and ironically. The third window of Emily's room looks west, towards The Evergreens, Austin's and Sue's equally large, but more fancifully Italianate house next door. In winter the houses are clearly visible to each other, although they are about a hundred yards apart. Even today, despite the straggling undergrowth, one can still discern the path between them. At the back was the carriage-house for the fine Dickinson carriages which, in later years, Mabel Loomis Todd was so pleased to ride about in around Amherst.

Upstairs, in Emily's bedroom, one of the white dresses she wore as ambiguous emblem of spiritual marriage and singleness hangs in the closet. It is a simple but elegant cotton summer dress, with a dropped waist, flat tucks and embroidery. It would not have required a corset. Those who have been victors 'Of tribulation' are 'Denoted by the White', Dickinson wrote; white is also her colour of sacrifice and death. The startlingly small, low table, only about eighteen inches square, where Dickinson wrote her poems (now in the Houghton Library of Harvard University, where it stands near O. A. Bullard's 1840 portrait of the three Dickinson children) is made of cherry-wood, and quite unmarked. The bow-front bedroom bureau where Lavinia found the booklets of poems after Emily's death is simple and elegant; the Dickinsons had good, expensive, rather classical taste, and seem not to have thrown out their American Georgian-style furniture when it was the fashion to redecorate in high Victorian style. On the ground floor of the

Homestead, to the right of the front door as one enters, was the library, Edward Dickinson's study, well stocked in Emily's day with newspapers, literary and cultural magazines, the Bible, legal tomes, standard literary texts and the modern novels which Edward Dickinson as father was not always certain his daughters should read.

When Edward Dickinson built the house next door for his son and daughter-in-law, he meant the proximity of The Homestead and The Evergreens to express some idea of a Dickinson dynasty, and for a brief while it did. In one of her earliest surviving poems, Dickinson wrote of Vinnie, her sister, and Sue, her beloved friend and sister-in-law:

> One Sister have I in our house,
> And one, a hedge away.
> There's only one recorded,
> But both belong to me.

At the time — about 1858 — when this was written, Sue had already begun to drop Emily and concentrate her considerable energies on becoming Amherst's best-known hostess. The pain of rejection so close, by the one person whom the Dickinsons had brought into their 'house', seems to have been acutely felt by Emily. The figure of a powerful, seductive woman appears several times in Dickinson's poetry, but not as a self-image. Rather, the 'lady', 'Cleopatra' or 'Egypt' (a nickname for Sue) is externalized. The workings of Sue's heart and mind are seen as having been unjustly withheld by her. And if Sue could not be addressed intimately, then no one outside the house could be trusted. 'Family' and 'Homestead' remained congruent for the Dickinsons. Austin acted out this symbolic identification in the 1870s and 1880s, when he fled from the house of his bad marriage back to the Homestead, visiting Emily and Vinnie daily, and taking his young son Gilbert with him. From 1882 he regularly met his lover Mabel Loomis Tood at the Homestead, with his sisters' approval. It is no wonder that the embittered Sue found the Homestead 'immoral'.

In Emily Dickinson's poetry, love for the father is subsumed in a larger knowledge of the suffering he causes. Looking at

her family, her family's church and her society, she saw what
Jacques Lacan has called the Name of the Father inscribed
everywhere. The Father particularly ruled the church. In New
England, from the 1820s onwards, Unitarian reform had been
making steady inroads in the Puritan inheritance which was
enshrined in the Congregationalist Church, but Amherst and
the Dickinsons (except for Emily) remained with the older
church. Edward, Austin, Vinnie and Sue all made declarations
of acceptance of Christ. Had Emily been concerned with
finding a less rigid theology, the Christian pragmatism of the
Unitarian Church would not have been notably different from
that expressed in many of her poems about the borderline of
death. Neither Dickinson nor the Unitarians believed that it
was possible to 'see the Infinite through finite eyes'.[5] When
Dickinson does look into a transcendent world, its timelessness
and infinite reproduction of the same inspire a sublime dread
in her:

> Behind Me – dips Eternity –
> Before Me – Immortality –
> Myself – the Term between –

'They say' that in heaven Christ 'Himself – Himself divers-
ify –/In Duplicate divine'. Dickinson does not care for
multiples. Meanwhile there is only one of the speaker, who is
isolated at a point in time in the vast sea of timelessness. She is
like the moon,

> A Crescent in the Sea –
> With Midnight to the North of Her –
> And Midnight to the South of Her –
> And Maelstrom – in the Sky –

Dickinson's speculative flights into the metaphysical sublime
are carried out by her own imagination; this awful scene, like a
three-dimensional version of an apocalyptic painting by John
Martin, has been produced by her. God the Father plays no
role in authenticating the vision. Play with proportion is one
of Dickinson's resources; it shows she can know the universe.

Without hope, whether in love or in belief, the firmament turns inside out in a nightmare of disproportion. In another poem,

> I saw no Way — The Heavens were stitched —
> I felt the Columns close —
> The Earth reversed her Hemispheres —
> I touched the Universe —

Then the universe withdraws, leaving her 'a Speck upon a Ball'. Now circumference marks not her ring of power, but the limit to which she is flung, rather like the mythic figures in Blake's Prophetic Books who are flung by the Father—God Urizen and his henchmen to the verge of Non-Entity. She 'Went out upon Circumference — Beyond the Dip of Bell —'.

Although she admired declarations of faith in other poets such as George Eliot and Elizabeth Barrett Browning, Dickinson never trusted the idea of God the Father. She engaged in what would now be called a patriarchal analysis, finding what she called in 'I never lost as much but twice' the 'Burglar — Banker — Father' consistently present in both the literal and symbolic Father. As usual, Dickinson samples various attitudes, but all express distance, anger and doubt. At best Dickinson's Father is an absent presence, teasingly withdrawn. Even if His light is delusive and dangerous, it is light: 'Better an ignis fatuus/Than no illume at all' (in 'Those — dying then'). Prayed to in need, He doesn't answer:

> Of Course — I prayed —
> And did God care?
> He cared as much as on the Air
> A Bird — had stamped her foot —

Heaven for Dickinson is often the Eden of sexual fulfilment, sometimes deliciously close: 'Come slowly — Eden!'. More often it is 'the interdicted Land' of 'Heaven — is what I cannot reach!'. Like a travelling circus, Heaven can be there yesterday and gone today:

> I've known a Heaven, like a Tent —
> To wrap its shining Yards —
> Pluck up its stakes, and disappear —

Once arrived at, Heaven is likely to reflect precisely the petty imagination of its local believers: 'I went to Heaven −/'Twas a small Town −'. This witty critique darkens when Dickinson reflects upon the power that has designed Heaven. He is 'A Force illegible' in 'All Circumstances are the Frame'; the mingling of absence and law is the structure for unknowing.

On earth, God manifests himself through death and through guilt, the 'phosphorus of God' which burns the sleeper in the nightmare poem 'Who is it seeks my Pillow Nights −'. God abducts those we love and carries them away, across the barrier from knowable into unknowable.

> I've seen a Dying Eye
> Run round and round a Room −
> In search of Something − as it seemed −

Then, at the moment of death, the eye is sadistically 'soldered down', without even being able to disclose what it was that ''Twere blessed to have seen −', let alone actually seeing it.

As Emily Dickinson suffered the debilitating deaths of Samuel Bowles in 1878, Rev. Charles Wadsworth in 1882, her mother also in 1882, her beloved nephew Gilbert in 1883, and Judge Lord 1884, her view of God hardened.

> Of God we ask one favor,
> That we may be forgiven −
> For what, he is presumed to know −
> The Crime, from us, is hidden −

In a brilliant and bitter condensed image, Dickinson concludes this late poem by remarking that God keeps us in the 'magic Prison' of a banal and constrained life because He is jealous of the heaven on earth that is human happiness. The prisoners adopt the values of the jailor: 'We reprimand the Happiness/ That too competes with Heaven'.

In Christian theology, Christ, the Son of God, softens the outlines of his forbidding Father. In one beautiful but hectically compact poem, Dickinson combines imagery of nurture, sexuality and language to report the wonder of Christ as 'loved Philology':

A Word made Flesh is seldom
And tremblingly partook
Nor then perhaps reported

In the tradition of female mysticism, Dickinson identifies with Christ. In one brief, passionate cry she addresses Christ as the figural emblem of her own suffering:

Jesus! Thy Crucifix
Enable thee to guess
The smaller size!

Yet she is sceptical of the Christ who is, after all, about his Father's business. In 'I shall know why − when Time is over −' it is Christ who attempts to explain human anguish 'in the fair schoolroom of the sky −'. In a comic poem, Dickinson remarks that 'God is a distant − stately Lover −' who uses Christ to carry out his 'Vicarious Courtship' of souls. In an old new England tale, John Alden sent Miles Standish to woo the fair Priscilla. But like Priscilla, the soul is likely to 'Choose the Envoy − and spurn the Groom −'.

Between Christ, who suffered, and God−Father who is the law, stands the mysterious figure of Dickinson's Master, the male beloved. In her pathetic and moving drafts of three letters to this unknown man (now generally thought to be Samuel Bowles), Dickinson begs to be allowed even a scrap of his presence. 'I used to think when I died − I could see you − so I died as fast as I could −' (*Letters*, II, p. 374). For a woman who did not express her feelings in public, the Master letters represent almost a courting of humiliation and shame:

Oh, did I offend it − ~~Didn't it want me to tell it the truth~~ Daisy − Daisy − offend it − who bends her smaller life to his (it's) meeker (lower) every day − who only asks − a task − ~~who~~ something to do for love of it.

(*Letters*, II, p. 391)

Even to mention love gives offence, yet she cannot stop herself from writing this broken plea. These were not words which Dickinson would have wanted Bowles's wife to see (or

the Rev. Charles Wadsworth's wife, if he was the Master).
Perhaps they survive because no final draft was ever sent. But
Dickinson embraces even the shame of her passion, because
that self-abnegation is part of passion too, and not to be
denied. In 'There is a Shame of Nobleness' she describes 'The
finer Shame of Ecstasy −/Convicted of Itself −'. In a later
poem, 'Shame is the shawl of Pink', it is the blush of shame
which raises us above the animal: 'Shame is the tint divine'.

CHAPTER FOUR

THE SPOKEN AND THE WRITTEN

They talk as slow as Legends grow
No mushroom is their mind
But foliage of sterility
Too stolid for the wind —
  ('They talk as slow as Legends grow')

You say 'Beyond your knowledge.' You would not jest with me, because I believe you — but Preceptor — you cannot mean it? All men say 'What' to me, but I thought it a fashion —
  (*Letters*, II, p. 415)

In the years of her maturity, Emily Dickinson expressed herself through silence — a curious kind of *written* silence. According to her contemporaries' norms of femininity, Emily Dickinson's silence was a social affront, the kind of affront noted by women at least as much as men. In terms of the nineteenth-century expansive rhetoric of secular and religious discourse, Dickinson's rhetoric of intense, compact address to her topic was an anomaly. Because it did not look like the work of published poets, it seemed unprofessional. Nor does Dickinson's rhetorical difference stop with her writing's address to knowledge. Within the poem, Dickinson enacts discontinuity and concentrates upon the individual, highly-charged word. This view of language was at odds with the then prevailing view, represented by Ralph Waldo Emerson's essay 'The Poet', in which Emerson expressed his confidence in the availability of the transcendent, universal symbol. By taking a different path from the psychological and symbolic modes which nineteenth-century writers were developing to represent broken selves, Dickinson also develops her own womanly rhetoric, 'silent' but fiercely directed through writing, able to endure the breaking of desire without sublimating desire itself (see Chapter 9).

Emily Dickinson recognized her literary vocation in adolescence. In April 1850, some months before her twentieth birthday, she wrote a long meditative letter to a friend, Jane Humphreys. The letter discusses religious doubt and literary ambition in a manner that indicates Dickinson saw a connection between them. This connection was one which the young aspiring writer felt would exclude her forever from the current religious and social discourse of New England society. Having begun a discussion of the religious revival in Amherst, Dickinson wrote:

How lonely this world is growing, something so desolate creeps over the spirit and we don't know it's name, and it wont go away, either Heaven is seeming greater, or Earth a great deal more small, or God is more 'Our Father,' and we feel our need increased. Christ is calling everyone here, all my companions have answered, even my darling Vinnie believes she loves, and trusts him, and I am standing alone in rebellion, and growing very careless.

(*Letters*, I, p. 94)

Emily wishes Jane were not so far away, because she wants her friend's reaction to a daring step she is in the process of taking:

I know you would be surprised, whether in pleasure, or disappointment it does'nt become me to say — I have dared to do strange things — bold things, and have asked no advice from any — I have heeded beautiful tempters, yet do not think I am wrong. . . . Oh Jennie, it would relieve me to tell you all, to sit down at your feet, and look in your eyes, and confess what *you only* shall know, an experience bitter, and sweet, but the sweet did so beguile me — and life has had an aim, and the world has been too precious for your poor — and striving sister!

(*Letters*, I, p. 95)

This striving has continued for months: 'The winter was all

one dream'. Nor does Dickinson wish to leave this 'sleep'. Then, switching to the terminology of a young girl's sewing and fancy embroidery 'works', she asks her 'sister' Jane to understand her new work.

What do you weave from all these threads, for I know you have'nt been idle the while I've been speaking to you, bring it nearer the window, and I will see, it's all wrong unless it has one gold thread in it, a long, big shining fibre which hides the others – and which will fade away into Heaven while you hold it, and from there come back to me. . . . – do you dream from all this what I mean? Nobody *thinks* of the joy, nobody *guesses* it, to all appearance old things are engrossing, and new ones are not revealed, but there *now* is nothing old, things are budding, and springing, and singing, and you rather think you are in a green grove, and it's branches that go, and come.

(*Letters*, I, p. 95)

In these passages, Emily Dickinson describes herself as in rebellion against God and Father. She feels baffled by the ease with which others have been able to accept the love of Christ the Son. Alone in her rebellion like Satan, she has also, Eve-like, been tempted. No other person seems to be involved in this sense of new purpose in the self; Dickinson doesn't appear to be describing even an idealized version of falling in love. The 'beaufitul tempters' are internal. As agent and object of her rebellious desires, she has dared 'do strange things'. Yet these same acts, 'sweet' and 'bitter' simultaneously, are the only things that give life an aim.

Where pleasure occurs is in a revelatory freshening of life. This 'joy' arises from the act which Dickinson describes by two metaphors – first, the 'gold thread' woven into cloth, and second, the months-long 'dream' or vision. In his biography of Emily Dickinson, Richard Sewall has suggested that this gold thread was Dickinson's awakening sense of literary vocation. Much of Dickinson's poetics is presaged by the 'gold thread' letter, whose terms reverberate through several other letters from the same period. Latin scholar Emily may even have been making a conscious or unconscious macaronic pun on 'text', since literary text and textile share the same Latin origin: *texere* is to weave; *textum* is a woven cloth or web and, in the rhetoric of Quintillian, it also means the texture of written composition. Thus Dickinson hopes to weave her texts, as her version of a young woman's 'work'.

The dream, a frequent nineteenth-century image for a poetic emotion, is not seen by Dickinson as an escape or as something less than reality; it is, if anything, a stronger alternative. Neither the dream metaphor nor the thread metaphor expresses a conflict within Dickinson, or (in terms of the act itself) competitiveness with others. The opposition described near the beginning of the letter was to do with Dickinson defying the socially approved transcendent route to happiness, and choosing another for herself. When Christ, as Dickinson remarks elsewhere in the letter, 'comes down to select his friends' (*Letters*, I, p. 94), those who choose not to join the elect must be the reprobate, and look out onto the earth rather than up to heaven. Dickinson's imagery doesn't invoke the language of quest, or draw attention to herself as Promethean hero; her joyous act simply seems to be an immediate and intense experience, whose pleasure is arrived at by means opposite to those taken by people who respond to the call of the Father. Also, while the evidence of 'change' is written all over the radiant faces of the freshly converted, Dickinson's independent act is going to have to be puzzled out with some care by her close, but very conventionally Christian, friend.

The 'gold thread' letter was preceded by one to Emily's other close girlfriend of the time, Abiah Root, in which Emily wrote, only partly humorously, about a 'tormentor' which has embraced 'and began to kiss me immoderately'. Since that first embrace this pleasant incubus has accompanied her everywhere 'and will tag me through life for all I know' (*Letters*, I, p. 87). In her playful discussion Dickinson has significantly separated writing from acts of will. She declares that this naughty tormentor makes a young girl give forth fiction and metaphor in an immoderate fashion:

let me tell you that these last thoughts are fictions – vain imaginations to lead astray foolish young women. They are flowers of speech, they

both *make*, and *tell* deliberate falsehoods, avoid them as the snake . . .
  (*Letters*, I, p. 88)

The flower of speech not only has a serpent under it (in an echo of Lady Macbeth), it is snake-like itself in its fiction-making power. The snake is, of course, sexually Satanic, as Dickinson wittily indicates, but it is also real, since Abiah has recently suffered a potentially dangerous snake-bite. The letter continues with its 'slant' or faceted writing, as Dickinson circles around her topic, approaching it from the different angles of various metaphors. What Abiah and she should be writing to each other about is 'something besides severe colds, and serpents' (Abiah had been having a bad cold). Nor are 'the gardens, and pretty strawberry beds' of feminine discourse quite right as the metaphor. 'It cant be a school-house, nor an Attorney at Law' (patriarchal territory). Dickinson concludes, as in many of her poems, with an approximation of likeness. 'Love for the absent dont *sound* like it, but try it, and see how it goes' (*Letters*, I, p. 88). In this letter at least, the function of metaphor is clearly communicative: to send love to Abiah, in whatever verbal way is most pleasurable, as a gift from 'Your very sincere, and *wicked* friend, Emily E. Dickinson'.

The gold thread letter was followed a month later by another of comparable intensity to Abiah, in which the two metaphors of dream and gold have been conflated into 'a *golden* dream, with eyes all the while wide open'. This dream has been dreamed 'from *to* and *fro*, and walking up, and down the same place that Satan hailed from' (*Letters*, I, p. 99). Dickinson is citing the Book of Job 1:7, in which Satan has been 'going to and fro in the earth, and . . . walking up and down in it'. In another admixture of Eve and Satan, Dickinson is locating where she has 'strayed', and she considers earth the appropriate Satanic habitation. She may have quoted the Book of Job as a covert allusion to God's cruel testing of his faithful servant Job, a testing which is not readily distinguishable from the actions of a devil.

Three years later Emily's writing was out in the open. She threw down a vivid challenge to her older brother Austin, who had evidently been trying his hand at mythological verse — or rather, as her letter shows, he had been giving himself the name of poet, with scant cause:

And Austin is a Poet, Austin writes a psalm. Out of the way, Pegasus, Olympus enough 'to him', and just say to those 'nine muses' that we have done with them!

Raised a living muse ourselves, worth the whole nine of them. Up, off, tramp!

(*Letters*, I, p. 235)

In these letters Dickinson initiated what would be for her a lifelong concern about the relation between writing and innate value. The pearls and precious gems of her metaphoric crown shine separately, while gold is her metonymic name for the wealth which is her poetic gift. Gold is a doubtful term for a Romantic poet such as William Blake because of its associations with oppressive power, but it can be a term of value for Dickinson so long as it has not been moulded into the currency of direct monetary exchange. In 'It was given to me by the Gods —', Dickinson describes her poetic gift as a literal gift, given 'by the Gods' (not by 'God'). Dickinson remarks that even as 'a little Girl', when she heard such words as 'rich' being spoken in social discourse, she had to smile:

> Rich! 'Twas Myself — was rich —
> To take the name of Gold
> And Gold to own — in solid Bars —
> The Difference — made me bold —

The child Dickinson's lucid awareness of the 'Difference' between the material and significatory use of gold gave her a defiant strength from early on. Her critique of the economics of literature in poems like 'Publication — is the Auction' was based upon her knowledge of a wealth which cannot be piled up in bars because it has value only in semiological terms, as a 'name'. If 'Gold' is the name she gives to the gift she has received, then she can be rich while also being poor. The world of poetry and the world of Mammon were often opposed in nineteenth-century poetry, with poetry the true value and material wealth the false. Dickinson converts not just 'wealth' but the less malleable terms 'Gold' and 'rich', and she doesn't use them to mean poetry or truth. They 'mean' whatever Dickinson's gift is, but that meaning can only be derived from reading all her writing. The gift has been given by the Gods, but 'Gold' is a name she has taken for her 'self'.

After she wrote the 'gold thread' letter recognizing the presence of her gift, Dickinson wrote the poems and letters which have come down to us. She was a prodigious producer of words. These words were, however, almost all written, and almost all of them were written in a private capacity. Her powerful sense of poetic vocation didn't extend to practising the profession of authorship as it was then understood. Dickinson didn't recite her poems in public and, in the absence of evidence to the contrary, she appears not to have recited them to friends either. Although there were lively evenings at The Evergreens in the 1850s, by the 1860s Emily Dickinson did not attend even family parties, and she ceased to go out in public. She played the piano, but not for groups. She spoke to guests whom she wanted to see, such as Thomas Wentworth Higginson, but he found her concentrated, highly metaphoric speech awesomely intense — too strong for even a literary lady. What Higginson was experiencing was written words — the charged, elliptical language of Dickinson's poems — uttered as speech without any modification. Only the famous ten poems were printed, and she did not publish articles or reviews. This public silence had a complex basis in Dickinson family relations, nineteenth-century gendering of literature, and prevailing poetic convention. Dickinson's failing eyesight was also a large, but inestimable, factor. The precise proportions in this cocktail of causality may never be settled. What is immediately striking, however, is just how noticeable Dickinson's *social* silence was to her contemporaries, whether or not they had read her manuscript poems.

Written language is what survives most readily from earlier cultures, mainly because it is meant to be preserved, and it can be copied. Lavinia Dickinson preserved her sister Emily's poems, had them copied, and got them to people who edited and printed them. Dickinson's relation to the written word has therefore survived well. Even if the poems were mangled by early editors, we do have them now, and Mabel Loomis Todd's prompt and vigorous research located many letters while their recipients were still alive. Indeed, those writings have become 'Dickinson', the poet we read. There is also, however, Dickinson the myth. In Dickinson's case, the provenance of the myth can be located with some accuracy.

That false self which has got between reader and poems since their first publication in 1890 arose directly out of Dickinson's relation to social discourse as her contemporaries understood it. The Dickinson myth crosses with her texts, but isn't congruent with them and cannot be generated from them alone. Had Dickinson's poems only been recovered long after the erasure of living memory (as was the case with the Puritan poet and minister Edward Taylor),[1] the myth could not have been generated solely from the texts.

The image of Emily Dickinson the eccentric old maid originated during her lifetime, and had already taken a powerful hold upon local imagination before the poems were published. In an age of female stereotypes, many men and women – though not all – accepted male views of the unfulfilled and odd old maid. Although Austin Dickinson always maintained that his sister Emily's life had followed an entirely natural course, others in Amherst were convinced they knew better. Conventional married women could use these prejudices to reinforce their own choice, while in the male version of such mutually reinforcing egotism, the husband could flatter his wife by emphasizing his choice of her for elevation to the married state. Thomas Wentworth Higginson's wife, for example, protected the uniqueness of her relation to her husband by deciding to interpret Dickinson's intensity as madness: 'Oh why do the insane so cling to you?' she said.[2] Literary man Joseph Lyman wrote distastefully detailed descriptions to his bride-to-be about how Lavinia had made advances to him seven years earlier (when Vinnie had been sixteen). By contrast, Emily was 'noble' but 'will probably [n]ever marry' (Sewall, I, pp. 138–40). The lesson is that women on either side of the gender norm — too sensual or too spiritual — could look forward to a life of celibacy. Lyman's fiancée could presumably rejoice in being the happy mediocrity in between. In Lyman's gender clichés we may hear the echo, a generation later, of Edward Dickinson's strictures on proper femininity in his letter to his fiancée Emily Norcross.

The availability of gender stereotypes also meant that women could use them against other women. In 1881, impressionable young Mabel Loomis Todd, whose astronomer husband had just been appointed to run the observatory at Amherst College, set about finding her place in local society. In Amherst, that meant getting invited to Sue and Austin Dickinson's and, in rare cases, getting into the Dickinson inner sanctum of the Homestead. A gossipy letter that Mabel Todd wrote soon after she met the Dickinsons expresses the full-blown myth:

I must tell you about the *character* of Amherst. It is a lady whom the people call the *Myth*. . . . She has not been outside of her own house in fifteen years, except to see a new church, when she crept out at night, & viewed it by moonlight. No one who calls upon her mother & sister ever see her, but she allows little children once in a great while, & one at a time, to come in. . . . She dresses wholly in white, & her mind is said to be perfectly wonderful. She writes finely, but no one *ever* sees her. Her sister, who was at Mrs Dickinson's party, invited me to come & sing to her mother sometime. . . . People tell me the *myth* will hear every note — she will hear, but unseen.[3]

Mabel Todd, repeating local received knowledge, notably doesn't locate Emily Dickinson's oddity in any mental derangement: 'her mind is said to be perfectly wonderful'. A year later, having read several gift-poems, which Emily had sent to her with flowers, Mabel would improve this view: 'She is in many respects a genius'.[4] The difficulty was also not exclusively attributable to Dickinson's single state, which isn't the object of comment, though Mabel alludes to it.

What seems to have caused considerable dismay was Emily Dickinson's persistent refusal to participate in feminine social discourse, several of whose norms are mentioned in Mabel Todd's letter. A lady — that is, a woman of the middle class or 'good family' – would be expected to give and receive social calls from other ladies. Married or single, she should be 'at home' at certain times of day, available to be called upon. She would be expected to attend church regularly, and to support the work of the church, through contributing her time, money, presence and piety. Her own charitable impulses would be channelled socially through groups of women like those who knitted socks for the Union soldiers. Apart from her own domestic management, a lady would also supervise and participate in home-related and, possibly, culture-related activities, from the local baking contest to the lyceum lecture of the larger town.[5]

The case of the old maid exaggerates that of the married lady. As someone perceived to have no value in herself, the old maid is meant to attain social value by her selfless usefulness to others, notably those younger, stronger and – in many cases – wealthier than herself. If she has wealth, she is expected to give it away, since she has no husband to take it from her. When that demand is implicitly or explicitly refused, social anger is directed at the non-giver. This structuring of the old maid is found throughout nineteenth-century literature; Emily Dickinson was reading about it while she was gradually becoming what society called an old maid. The structures were specific, as Sandra Gilbert and Susan Gubar note in *The Madwoman in the Attic*. In Charles Dickens's *Great Expectations*, Pip assumes that the rich old maid Miss Havisham has been giving him the money he has used to make himself a gentleman. When he learns that she isn't his benefactress, and that her sponsorship of Estella has not been for his sake either, he is horrified. The novelist is horrified too. A rich, powerful old maid is dangerous. Miss Havisham is a witch, and Dickens has her burnt alive, still wearing the white gown in which she had been abandoned at the altar decades before. Her death is, of course, her own fault.

A process of conversion of the old maid's low value into high sentiment can be seen at work in some women's writing, but the shift is by no means complete. In George Eliot's narrative and dialogue poem 'Agatha' (1869), which Emily Dickinson read, the old maid seems to have to be excessively contained by the poem before her virtues are accepted. Already miniaturized by the frame of a German, Catholic, picturesque setting, the old maid Agatha is also tiny, aged, weak and poor. Yet she is of use:

> in the big farm-house
> When cloth comes home from weaving, the good wife
> Cuts me a piece, – this very gown, – and says:
> 'Here Agatha, you old maid, you have time
> To pray for Hans who is gone soldiering.
> The saints might help him, and they have much to do,
> 'Twere well they were besought to think of him.'
> She spoke half jesting, but I pray, I pray
> For poor young Hans. I take it much to heart
> That other people are worse off than I, –
> I ease my soul with praying for them all.[6]

Poor Agatha feels others are poorer than she, because she has the gift of prayer. George Eliot's tone is curious; she spells out the mockery by the fecund at some length; later in the poem a group of boisterous youths plan to 'play some friendly trick/On three old maids' (though they don't). While criticizing society's dismissive mockery of the Agathas of this world, Eliot reproduces it by miniaturization and the picturesque. The Catholic period setting of 'Agatha' does eventually prove to have more than an 'exotic' function, in that the poem concludes that an unfecund Mary can also be a mother: 'bless the aged mother-maiden!' sing the youths. Agatha's role is to interpose ''Twixt faulty folk and God'; she is a kind of white witch. Perhaps the reasons for the poem's uncomfortable mixture of respect and condescension can be found, as with Dickens, in a covert defence of the author's own position. George Eliot was sexually active (she had been living with G. H. Lewes for fifteen years when she wrote 'Agatha'), but she wasn't married and it was out of the question for her to have children. 'Agatha' defends both the usefulness and powers of the childless woman, while preserving the conventional view of the old maid. No one would confuse the author of 'Agatha' with her character. George Eliot has fallen into the trap by which a woman writer retains 'good' gender qualities for herself, while displacing 'bad' qualities on to a cliché image whose ultimate basis is misogynist.

The Dickinsons were one of the two most important families in Amherst, so the silence and invisibility of the oldest Dickinson daughter was perceived as at best an abnegation of duty and at worst a social 'cut'. Emily Dickinson kept herself to herself, in the expressive colloquial phrase. While Vinnie, with her hooked nose and sharp tongue, fulfilled social expectations of the old maid, the invisible and silent Emily had the potential to be infinitely more dangerous, since she accepted her dangerousness.

Well aware that she would have been on the receiving end of the terrible witch-huntings and witch-burnings of seventeenth-century New England,[7] Dickinson seizes the name 'witch' for the woman poet just as boldly as she seizes the name 'queen'. Witchcraft is womanly poetic work: in 'I think I was enchanted', a poem about the discovery of poetic vocation, Dickinson swears to return, if threatened, to the 'Tomes of solid witchcraft' that Elizabeth Barrett Browning has written.

'Witchcraft was hung, in History', one late poem begins,

> But History and I
> Find all the Witchcraft that we need
> Around us, every Day.

'Witchcraft has not a Pedigree', Dickinson remarks in another poem; it is coeval with the vital breath of life itself:

> 'Tis early as our Breath
> And mourners meet it going out
> The moment of our death —

The Mabel Todd who wrote the 1881 'myth' letter about Emily Dickinson was a socially insecure young woman. An accomplished pianist and singer with artistic leanings, and very attractive, Mabel Todd came nonetheless from a borderline artisan-middle-class family without much money or the attention to female education that marked the New England upper middle class. Her pleasure at penetrating into the Sue Dickinson salon was tempered by the fact that the Dickinson family's 'artistic' member refused to receive her as a lady caller, wouldn't talk to her, and would not even appear in the same room.

The act of gift-giving is heavily fictionalized by Mabel Todd. Emily Dickinson's everyday generosity provoked Mabel's most vivid sketches of bizarre behaviour: the Myth does let children into the Homestead and gives them her cakes, 'but more often she lets down the sweetmeat by a string, out of a window, to them.'[8] According to the notes made by Mabel's daughter Millicent Todd Bingham, Emily's gifts to children were indeed habitual. The cakes lowered, witch-like, on a string, were a fabrication, though one which her mother (and others) found it amusing to believe. 'Isn't that like a book?' Mabel Todd exclaimed at the end of her anecdote. Mabel will feel safer if this strange Dickinson can be shrunk into a local version of a Dickens grotesque. In fact, Emily Dickinson's generosity of heart extended to more than cakes. During the long years of the 'war between the houses' caused by the unhappy marriage of Austin and Sue, Emily alone remained consistently thoughtful and loving to all parties.

In mid and late nineteenth-century New England, social discourse played a role whose importance is difficult to assess today, so greatly have our modes of communication changed. Emily Dickinson lived in an age of speech, an age of great public orators and constant private conversation. A look at this world of speech may serve to point up the shape of Dickinson's silence. By definition, the orator's effect depended upon his personal presence. 'Live' performance was the only kind of performance there was. Thus, despite the great distances of the United States, a charismatic preacher such as the Rev. Charles Wadsworth of Philadelphia could gain a national reputation through the power of his oratory. A high point of the Dickinson sisters' two-week stay in Philadelphia in 1855 would have been a visit to their hosts' church, where Wadsworth was minister. A civilized person's trip would otherwise not have been complete. But the mid nineteenth century was perhaps the last great age of spoken social discourse. Most of the inventions of the late nineteenth century were concerned with the mechanical reproduction of discourse or its movement through space: the telegraph, the telephone, the phonograph and, finally, the motion picture. The daguerrotype, the sensation of the 1840s and 1850s, had introduced the mechanical reproduction of three-dimensional illusion; Dickinson's refusal to be photographed after her seventeenth birthday is part of her economy of signification; by visual silence she indicated her dislike of reproductions of self.

To speak generally, the nineteenth century was also an age of expansion — of scientific discovery, exploration, finance capital and imperialism. Although its belief in a direct line of descent back to the Biblical creation was broken by the publication of Darwin's *The Origin of Species* in 1858, the historical sense of the Victorian era remained teleological; human history was seen to have a purpose and a goal. The style of American oratory was part of this expansive sensibility, offering an assurance that language could express what society needed to have expressed, filling space with a convincing rhetoric, whether of assurance or anathema, and filling time with its length. Novels in the realist tradition positioned their questioning inside a comparable access to knowledge. In philosophical terms, the mid and late nineteenth century was an age of entelechy.

Emily Dickinson grew up in this world. In a town like Amherst, sermons, lectures and political speeches were major social events. Literature was meant to be read rhetorically. The standard rhetorical textbooks of Dickinson's girlhood, such as Ebenezer Porter's *Rhetorical Reader* (Amherst Academy) and Newman's *Rhetoric* (required for the senior students at Mount Holyoke), directed their readers towards developing effective argument, with emphasis upon oratorical skill and elocution. Dickinson's Latin textbook, *A Grammar of the Latin Language: for the Use of Schools and College* by Stoddard and Andrews (1843), concluded with a full list of classical rhetorical devices.[9] Such a rhetorical poetics had been challenged by — among others — Wordsworth in the Preface to the second edition of

Lyrical Ballads (1800), but it persisted in standard American texts, even when some selections were made from near-contemporary writers.

Secular oratory was personified in Amherst by Edward Dickinson; Emily experienced its power at home in her father's house. A follower of the great Whig orator Daniel Webster, Edward Dickinson appears to have adopted his mentor's rhetoric as well as his politics. Indeed the two were inseparable. The exordium (which defined the audience), the statement of the case, the proof and the conclusion, all followed a classical pattern modified in the United States by the addition of Biblical tags. Known forms gave strength to known themes in this rhetoric of the law of the Father. The horror felt in communities like Springfield and Amherst towards Abolitionist orators arose, I suspect, not because the locals favoured slavery, but because the abolitionists broke a basic rule of the rhetoric of entelechy, namely that oratory should be structured so as to underwrite the idea of completeness. A rhetoric which could consider extra-legal action or encourage the possible break-up of the Union was profoundly threatening to a form of thought which assumed speech could gain agreement. It is not surprising that the dark divisions pointed up by Melville made his later novels unacceptable to such a society; if the problem did not arise with Dickinson, it is because her poems of division and spiritual doubt were largely kept out of the first selections of her work.

A look at some of the social discourse of the winter season 1838–9 in Boston may give some idea of the centrality of speech for New England society. Ralph Waldo Emerson was delivering his lecture series 'The Present Age' every Wednesday from December through to February (the year before, he had delivered his 'Human Life' series). Bronson Alcott, another member of the Transcendentalist group, was lecturing on 'Interpretations of Christianity' every Sunday, beginning in November. In October, Margaret Fuller, teacher, writer, feminist and member of the Transcendentalist group, began her series of female 'conversations' with twenty-five women by subscription, with another series to follow in spring 1840.

On a private level, the Transcendental Club was meeting in various homes.

Meanwhile, on Sundays, people expected a good sermon, well researched, satisfying audience expectations, moving, well delivered, and long enough to cover several topics. Letters of this period, including Dickinson's, are sprinkled with informal reviews of sermon performances. In 1833 Margaret Fuller had written that she was 'deeply interested in the morning sermon which was on the text — Work out your salvation with fear and trembling —'. The service resumed in the afternoon, when Fuller found the sermon 'did not come home to my previously unfinished trains of thought —'. Elocution came in for comment: 'He does not read the hymns well. His emphasis is faulty, cadences governed by no rule and manner much too rapid, indeed very conversational.'[10]

In her youthful sermon reviews, Dickinson comments only on the performative person — the sense of full presence. In 1853, 'We had such a splendid sermon from that Prof Park' (Rev. Edwards Amasa Park):

The [Amherst] students and chapel people all came, to our church, and it was very full, and still — so still, the buzzing of a fly would have boomed like a cannon. And when it was all over, and that wonderful man sat down, people stared at each other, and looked as wan and wild, as if they had seen a spirit, and wondered they had not died.

   (*Letters*, I, p. 272)

Dickinson speaks consistently as 'we' in these appreciations; to the extent she can respond to the part of the rhetorical contract which is the presence of the charismatic speaker, she can be part of the group. At Mount Holyoke she refused to speak when asked to avow Christ, and so she became a 'no-hoper'. When, a few years later, Dickinson ceased to 'keep the Sabbath by going to church' (as she began one poem), she also departed from a major area of shared social discourse of her time.

Both the power and the eventual limitations of public oratory were tested in the public arena by the Civil War. Abraham Lincoln offered an epitome of rhetorical technique and an implicit farewell to its expansive terms when he delivered the Gettysburg Address. Although it was criticized at the time for its undignified brevity, the Gettysburg Address showed that traditional oratory could rise to the occasion of mass carnage and offer a profoundly moving response. Lincoln's famous lines, 'We cannot dedicate, we cannot consecrate, we cannot hallow this ground', apply the classical rhetorical trope of anaphora, or repeated beginning, to the issue of dedicating the cemetery for the war dead. Other Civil War literature was equally rhetorical. Julia Ward Howe's 'The Battle Hymn of the Republic' applied the language of the apocalypse to the situation of the war, with electrifying rhetorical effect, showing incidentally that American women could write public poetry when they used public rhetoric. Edmund Clarence Stedman's 'Wanted − A Man', for some decades thought to be one of the finer poems to have come out of the war, concluded each stanza with the vocative, highly rhetorical call, 'Abraham Lincoln give us a MAN!' 'O Captain! My Captain!', Walt Whitman's deliberately conventional 'popular' elegy to Lincoln, is constructed around a similar repeated vocative, anaphorically placed at the beginning of each stanza.

Whitman's unconventional poetry also took over many essential aspects of public discourse. His use of anaphora as the organizing device for his free verse lines links his poetry firmly to the oratorical tradition. The 'breath' measure of the Whitman line is the actual or hyperbolical acting out of recitation on the page. The free, ever-expanding length of the Whitman poem is a powerful formal expression of entelechy; sooner or later, as the poem spreads out over silence, it will be possible to say anything without let or hindrance.

There is something slightly Dickinsonian about the Gettysburg Address. Instead of the President soothing and reinforcing the audience over a period of an hour or two with his charismatic personal presence and eloquent delivery, he spoke for less than five minutes. A good part of the power of the address came from the silence surrounding it. Lincoln had shown that rhetorical speech could fulfil its public task of consoling and dedicating without needing to fill space with assurance. As a presenceless presence, the address begins to come near to Dickinson's own silent rhetoric. It may also serve to remind us that Dickinson was, in her own silent way, a rhetorical poet.

American women were not slow to notice that those who were excluded from both pulpit and public platform were also effectively excluded from public action. Until the late 1830s American women faced social ignominy if they tried to break out of their proper province of the home and speak in public. However, the situation changed dramatically, at least as far as secular discourse was concerned, during the years of Emily Dickinson's youth. The breakthrough occurred with women's moral involvement with the abolition of slavery, when they concluded that only a mass public presentation of their views could bring about change. In 1837, Sarah and Angelina Grimké, two sisters from South Carolina, gave a series of anti-slavery parlour talks to women in New York. They found that men were also attending, making the talks in effect public. For a lecture tour of New England in 1837–8, the sisters gained a public platform, and in February 1838, Angelina Grimké twice addressed the Massachusetts State Legislature, a hitherto unprecedented access to public oratory for a woman. It was during this period that Angelina made the connection between the disenfranchisement of blacks and the disenfranchisement of women which was to provide the ideological base for the new American women's equal rights movement a decade later.[11]

When Margaret Fuller was setting up her less overtly political 'conversations' in Boston the following autumn (1839), she stressed the importance of public speaking for women. Fuller felt that the give and take of public debate was necessary:

To systematize thought and give a precision in which our sex are so deficient, chiefly, I think, because they have so few inducements to test and classify what they receive.[12]

Women should be prepared to bear their part, to question, to define, to state and examine their opinions. Fuller was emphasizing the importance of discourse, public rhetoric, exchange of views – what we would now call feedback – in

Emily as Lavinia remembered her

Edward Dickinson

Emily, Justin and Lavinia Dickinson, 1840

Emily Dickinson's room

The Homestead, East Facade

Front door of the Dickinson Homestead   The Evergreens

The path to the Evergreens today

Austin and Lavinia Dickinson

Susan Gilbert Dickinson

Lavinia Dickinson, 1896

Emily Dickinson's
white dress

Silhouettes of Dickinson family, 1847

Mt. Holyoke Female Seminary

Amherst Common before 1880

Amity Street, Amherst. Amherst Academy to left

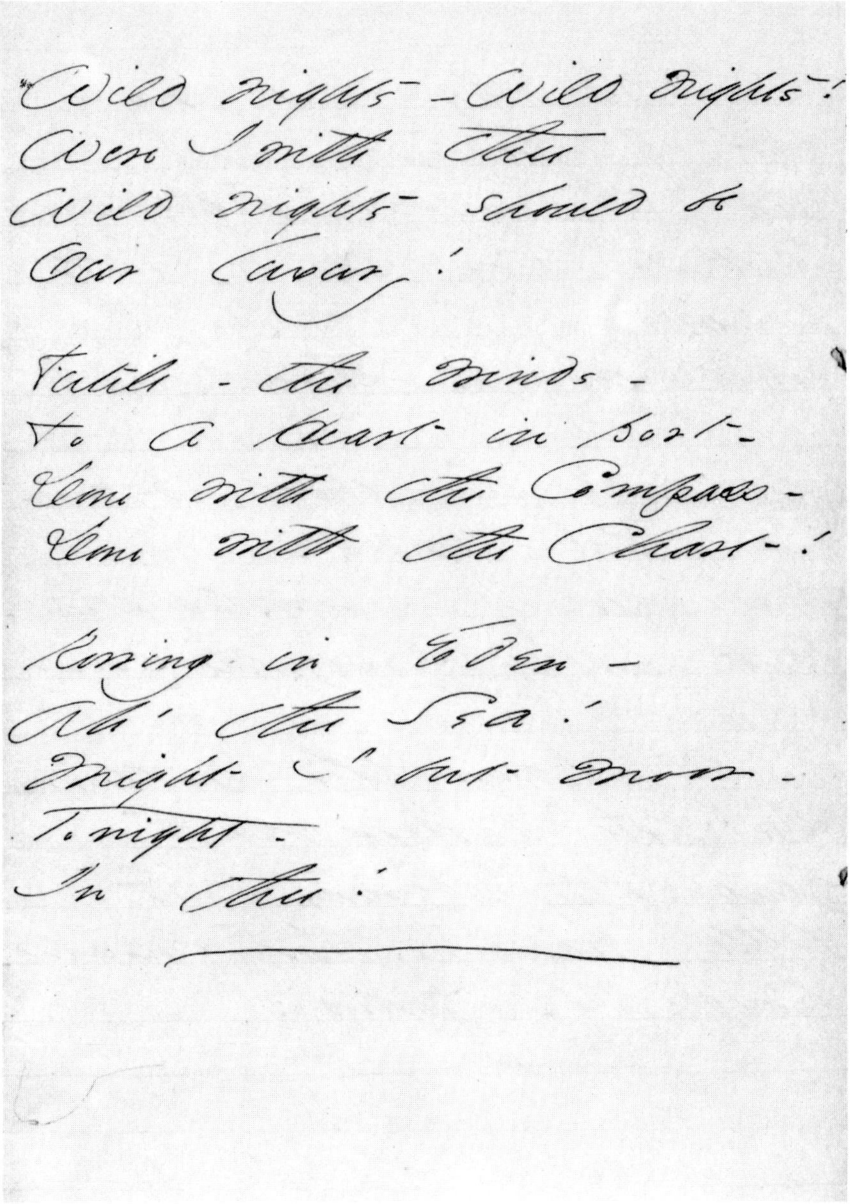
Wild Nights - Wild Nights!
Were I with thee
Wild Nights should be
Our Luxury!

Futile - the Winds -
To a Heart in port -
Done with the Compass -
Done with the Chart!

Rowing in Eden -
Ah, the Sea!
Might I but moor -
Tonight -
In Thee!

Manuscript of 'Wild Nights – Wild Nights!'

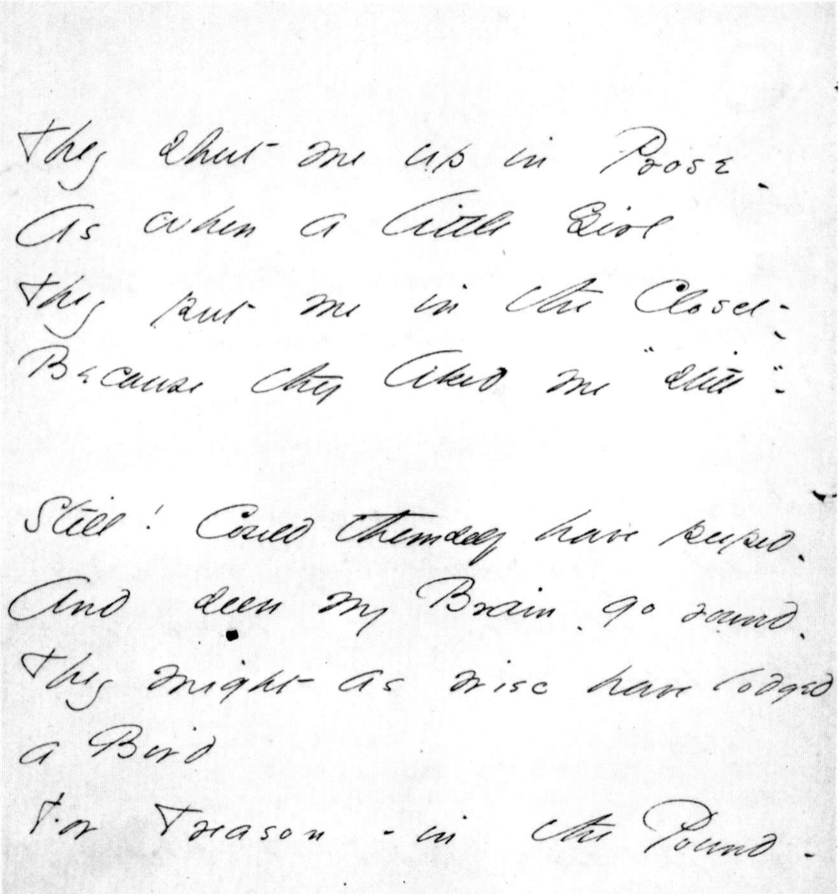

They shut me up in Prose –
As when a little Girl
They put me in the Closet –
Because they liked me "still" –

Still! Could themself have peeped –
And seen my Brain – go round –
They might as wise have lodged
a Bird
For Treason – in the Pound –

Himself has but to will
And easy, as a Star
+Look down opon Captivity –
And laugh – No more have I –
+ Abolish his –

Manuscript of 'They shut Me up in Prose' – showing revision

developing the female mind. As Fuller saw it in *Woman in the Nineteenth Century* (1845), the higher education which middle-class white American women were beginning to get in the 1840s was necessary to teach them discipline and the ability to categorize. These qualities were, for Fuller, prerequisites for civic responsibility.

Building upon the social acceptance of woman as a moral force within the home, mid-century women writers seized upon the opportunity to use their skills to address public moral issues. Having gained acceptance in the feminine-gendered genres of lyric and sentimental or didactic fiction, they extended these genres to public matters. Even when they did not make speeches, they rhetorically addressed their audience in such a manner as to convince them of the rightness of a cause. So the woman's voice made itself heard in democratic debate. Along with Howe's 'Battle Hymn of the Republic', among the most famous instances of such written female public rhetoric were Harriet Beecher Stowe's *Uncle Tom's Cabin* (1852), which adapted sentimental melodrama to the abolitionist cause, and her factual compilation *The Key to Uncle Tom's Cabin* (1853), which sought to convince critics that her fiction was true — that is, verifiable.

In 1884, Dickinson's friend Helen Hunt Jackson wrote a best-selling sentimental novel, *Ramona*, about the mistreatment of the California Mission Indians. Like Stowe a long generation earlier, Jackson backed up her fictional allegations with a 'masculine' factual account, except that the damning indictment came first, and the fiction was written to move the hearts which statistics had left untouched. Dickinson read *Ramona*, but her appreciative comment to Jackson was ambiguous: 'Pity me, however, I have finished Ramona. Would that like Shakespeare, it were just published!' (*Letters*, III, p. 867). Dickinson is saying that though she would have liked to stay longer in the world of *Ramona*, it is not a book which, like Shakespeare, will always seem 'just published'. She touches discreetly — almost invisibly — on one of the problems of all politically committed writing. A book which is too exclusively about its professed topic is limited by the contemporary range of the topic; when the issue is 'finished', so is the book.

Dickinson's writerly silence needs to be distinguished from the male social habit of solitude. Familiar to American readers through the literary image of bachelorhood in Washington Irving and in Ik Marvel's *Reveries of a Bachelor* (a favourite novel of the young Emily) the isolated male became part of the transcendental ethos. In 'The American Scholar' (1837) Emerson had advanced an image of the American scholar as solitary and, at least in part, the life of Thoreau and Thoreau's *Walden* expressed a need for withdrawal from a materialistic society. In 'Literary Ethics', an 1838 address developed from 'The American Scholar', Emerson told the members of the Literary Societies of Dartmouth College that the scholar 'must embrace solitude as a bride. He must have his glees and his glooms alone.'[13] The male writer may embrace solitude in a different way from a woman; he can be praised for having chosen it, and his choice rewards solitude. To criticise this stance it is not necessary to adduce Emerson's own extremely busy public life at this time, or to point out that he enjoyed an essentially suburban solitude created by a household run according to his needs. Elsewhere in 'Literary Ethics' Emerson argues that the reason for withdrawal is to give the scholar confidence in his ability to speak to, and for, the present. When the cultivated but reserved man, 'sitting silent, admires the miracle of free, impassioned, extempore speech, in the man addressing an assembly', he feels at first that this 'state of being and power' is 'unlike his own'. But if he permits 'his own emotion' to flow out in speech,

Once embarked . . . he finds it just as easy and natural to speak — to speak with thoughts, with pictures, with rhythmical balance of sentences, — as it was to sit silent; for, it needs not to do, but to suffer; he only adjusts himself to the free spirit which gladly utters itself through him; and motion is as easy as rest.

(*Essays and Lectures*, p. 101)

Because Emerson believes in a direct flow from 'the free spirit' through the man to a language of social discourse, the speaker naturally need only trust his utterance to speak truly.

By not joining in social discourse, Dickinson separated her writing from the Emersonian scholar and the public rhetoric of entelechy, or the assumption of the availability of completeness. Her silence was not, however, simply a declaration for a womanly language. In mid and late nineteenth-century America, what then seemed to be the progressive elements in women's writing and culture were entering into the hitherto masculine discursive mode. They did so with considerable success, as Helen Hunt Jackson's career shows. The women's rights movement and the women abolitionist orators, such as the Grimké sisters and Sojourner Truth, were genuine agents of change.

Was Dickinson's silence merely traditionally feminine, the product of values of reticence and class confidence? While the early date of the 'gold thread' letter makes it impossible to see her poetry as compensation for not getting married, she did write in the acceptably feminine genres of the lyric poem and the private letter. Her life, with its few externals, looks like that of the dutiful daughter of an earlier age. Certainly Sue Dickinson took the opportunity of writing her sister-in-law's obituary to advance a theory that Emily's life had fulfilled the traditional ideals of delicate, homebound womanhood:

The 'mesh' of her soul, as Browning calls the body, was too rare, and the sacred quiet of her own home proved the fit atmosphere for her worth and work. All that must be inviolate. One can only speak of 'duties beautifully done;' of . . . her quick and rich response to all who rejoiced or suffered at home, or among her wide circle of friends the world over. This side of her nature was to her the real entity in which she rested, so simple and strong was her instinct that a woman's hearthstone is her shrine.[14]

Or was her silence simply the result of one of those personal factors, such as shyness or poor eyesight, to which the critic can never gain full access?

None of these explanations looks likely to be the reason for the configuration of Dickinson's poetry. Too many conveniently satisfy conventions external to the poet herself, and her silence was not only an external habit. For her, it was integral to the poetic act. The split between the spoken and the written in Dickinson goes much deeper, past biography, down to the way she conceives of language. For Dickinson, knowledge was written. Modern poetry is, of course, also written, but we read it as if it were spoken. Historically, the lyric, ballad and epic were memorized and recited long before they were written down, and some kinds of poetry, such as ballad and popular song, still persist mainly in memorized form. We still habitually describe a poet's 'voice' or remark that he or she 'says', 'declares' or 'asserts'. Poetry readings and — in this century — recordings are part of the poet's presentation of his or her work. Some poets like Allen Ginsberg are, in effect, orators, their personal presence being essential for the full impact of the work. New movements in poetry regularly claim that they are returning poetry to its authentic basis in human speech.

Dickinson reverses these priorities. Her poetry puts writing first. When she makes explicit distinctions between written and spoken language, she strongly favours the former. It is not only that spoken language is ephemeral, while writing endures. The spoken is quite powerful enough once it is uttered. As Dickinson wrote, 'A man may make a Remark/In itself — a quiet thing', only to have that remark ignite something 'dormant'. In a reversal of the usual view, Dickinson associates speech with falsehood, and writing with truth. The falsity of speech is not just found in unpleasant instances. It is innate. In 'If What we could —', Dickinson writes:

> It is the Ultimate of Talk —
> The impotence to Tell —

Dickinson doesn't deny that direct and unambiguous personal presence which both Fuller and Higginson (in a memoir in *Contemporaries* of the abolitionist orator William Lloyd Garrison) admire in spoken language, but writes that that kind of self is superficial. There seems to be a critique of a fixed self, or selfhood, in Dickinson's preference for writing. For her, writing isn't the imperial self making a speech to convince its audience. Writing is undertaken on behalf of the topic which it is addressing, as if it is necessary to know as much as possible about that topic in as small a space as possible. Dickinson's 'writing' is not, as Emerson would have it in 'The Poet' and 'Literary Ethics', a direct flow from the spirit through man to society. For her, 'slant' or metaphorical writing is the only way to write accurately, because the truth is never obvious. It must be sought out inside language. If the person writing is a woman, there could not in any case be a direct flow from the spirit to the woman to a receptive society, because the woman would encounter social gendering.

At its best, according to Dickinson, typical feminine speech is prattle which — for a woman writer — insidiously locates the womanly in the socially gendered feminine. It is significant that Emerson doesn't use female examples when he discusses the free flow of the spirit into speech, nor does he use female examples in general. Although he certainly had heard such speech during his friendship with Fuller, the feminine *type* was of triviality. The 'Gentlewomen' of Dickinson's poem, 'What Soft — Cherubic Creatures —', utter their 'Dimity Convictions' and feel only a snobbish horror 'Of freckled Human Nature', of the kind that Dickinson, and most of the rest of us, exhibit. At its worst, speech — perhaps Sue Dickinson's speech — inflicts deep wounds. One poem begins:

> She dealt her pretty words like Blades —
> How glittering they shone —
> And every One unbared a Nerve
> Or wantoned with a Bone —

It is 'not Steel's Affair' to worry if it cuts. 'To Ache is human — not polite —'; since 'a vulgar grimace' might offend the lady, the best response for the victim is to die quietly. As the instrument of convention, speech wounds those who do not fit: 'All men say "What" to me'.

'They talk as slow as Legends grow', Dickinson begins another poem about speech. 'Legends', with its connotations of false fictions, does not play a positive role in Dickinson, particularly when the legend-makers are not poets but gossips.

Dickinson concludes her poem using the simile of predictable narrative to describe a kind of failure of futurity:

> They laugh as wise as Plots of Wit
> Predestined to unfold
> The point with bland prevision
> Portentously untold.

Their laughter is like the conclusion to a hackneyed mystery story; the secret is merely something that hasn't been talked about yet. There's no 'news' in such tales. 'Predestined' and 'portentous' link the empty predictability of gossip with sacred speech, the implication being that there, too, we all know what the conclusion is going to be.

'This World is not Conclusion', one of Dickinson's most important poems about belief, begins by offering the hope that there is a world beyond, a spiritual existence. As often in Dickinson, the metaphysical is signalled by music rather than speech. Then, bit by bit, her poem inexorably undermines all bases for faith. Sermons attempt to fill the void only with patriarchal noise:

> Much Gesture, from the Pulpit —
> Strong Hallelujahs roll —
> Narcotics cannot still the Tooth
> That nibbles at the soul —

For Dickinson here, as for Marx, religion is the opium of the people. But balm doesn't cure disease. Dickinson's in-biting tooth is one of the great poetic images of spiritual torment, comparable in intensity to Herbert's description of inner conflict in 'Affliction', in which he writes, 'My thoughts are all a case of knives'. In Herbert's poem faith finally returns; in Dickinson's, the last image is of the silent gnawing of doubt.

The glib public rhetoric of faith arouses some of Dickinson's sharpest sardonic responses:

> He preached upon 'Breadth' till it argued him narrow —
> The Broad are too Broad to define
> And of 'Truth' until it proclaimed him a Liar —
> The Truth never flaunted a Sign —

The facile use of abstractions is, for Dickinson, one of the hallmarks of false public speech. She has withdrawn from the discursive compact of her day, in which emotions and abstractions are known and need only be ornamented by image or exemplary tale. Dickinson does believe that there is such a thing as Truth — and here she differs from most modern writers — but the signs of Truth are not 'flaunted'. Those who preach as if they have a purchase on truth are actually 'counterfeits'. In another use of the 'gold' image, glib preachers are like 'Pyrites' (fool's gold) which true gold 'would shun'. Even Jesus, Dickinson remarks tartly in her last line, would feel 'confusion' if He were to meet 'so enabled a Man!'

Dickinson's poem 'Title divine — is mine!' deals with speech as it is influenced by gender. It begins triumphantly with a distinction between spiritual and material titles:

> Title divine — is mine!
> The Wife — without the Sign!
> Acute Degree — conferred on me —
> Empress of Calvary!

The speaker has been

> Betrothed — without the swoon
> God sends us Women —

Freed from socially gendered courtship, she and her lover will meet 'Garnet to Garnet', and 'Gold to Gold' — both key Dickinson images of creative ecstasy. They are also images of like next to like (this poem was sent to two people, Samuel Bowles and Sue Dickinson). Instead of being a transition from one state in life to another, the speaker's wedding eradicates both singleness and wifedom. Dickinson's speaker declares that her existence will consist only of the bridal day: 'Born — Bridalled — Shrouded —/In a Day —'. This is a 'Tri Victory'; Dickinson gives her coinage a line to itself. Then the exultant progress of the poem halts:

> 'My Husband' — women say —
> Stroking the Melody —
> Is *this* — the way?

Women 'stroke' the phrase, denoting possession, as they would stroke a pet. Dickinson's speaker has been wed without the explicit, outward 'Sign'. Lacking the literal 'Crown', she is by that lack made Empress of Calvary rather than of someone's household. Dickinson ends the poem with a sarcastic question: 'Is *this* — the way?' The coy, possessive phrase clearly is not the 'way' Dickinson has chosen, either in life or in art. Yet the meaning of 'this' is not entirely unambiguous. Indeed, the poem has implied that no sign should be completely outward. There's just a hint that Dickinson is also asking whether her own Christ-like way is, after all, 'the way'.

Dickinson's dislike of spoken language arises, then, from what she considers to be two different schema of signification: spoken public language consists of certitude, fixed perspective, convention, the social bargain struck between speaker and listener. Since gender roles are part of the contemporary social compact, speech enacts gender in its worst, most limiting form. Spoken language is where society utters its lies. For Dickinson, that which is not spoken partakes of a second schema, one involving ambiguity and truth, or perhaps an ambiguity which is akin to truth. Its rhetoric must derive from linguistic history, since it is comprehensible to us, but it argues without flow. It is highly condensed and elliptical, constructing its own lattices and diadems of metaphor without too much regard for received meaning.

When Dickinson constructs a verbal frame in which knowledge can grow, she usually tries out several perspectives in different poems. This is her practice when she addresses issues connected with death, the metaphysical, or houses. When the issue is language itself, she does not allow much speculative leeway. There are some exceptions, but these prove the rule. Dickinson's relatively few dialogue poems, for example, are often fairly perfunctory dialogues between personifications or abstractions, as in 'Death is a Dialogue between/The Spirit and the Dust.' Lovers who are close can speak. Or the speakers may talk frankly because both are dead, as in 'I died for Beauty —'. Or one will die soon, as in 'We talked as Girls do —', in which the girls' charming speculation about their future is cut short by death.

Dickinson's relatively unvarying stance on speech resembles the firm line she takes about the Father, and it may well derive from an analysis of patriarchal control of social discourse. Yet, while her critique of patriarchy is readily recognizable today, her radical reworking of linguistic priorities is much less familiar. Dickinson has been drawing a complex set of connections between the spoken, social convention, 'presence', wholeness, the Law of the Father, unexamined abstractions, lies and social gendering. Social discourse also encourages a transcendent symbolism without 'knowing' that transcendence. Dickinson draws another set of connections between writing, chosen silence, truth, ambiguity, specificity, the unframed, the female, desire and 'difference'. In these formulations she has mapped out with prophetic accuracy the areas addressed in some of this century's continuing attacks on the assumptions of traditional philosophy, as well as marking some spaces where no theorist has yet trod. Dickinson's poetry crosses with modern theory in Derrida's earlier works *Writing and Difference* and *Of Grammatology*, and in some aspects of Freud's thoughts. If I mention these theorists, it is not in order to read Dickinson in terms of Derrida or Freud. But my reading of these later thinkers has alerted me to just how inclusive and original Dickinson's discoveries are.

Derrida's theory has been elaborated out of loathing for transcendent presence. Like Dickinson, he finds writing more likely to represent experience accurately than speech, even though the historical precedence of speech has encouraged philosophers to date falsehood from the introduction of writing.[15] Derrida distinguishes between Logos or the Word of God, and writing, and identifies the spoken with the former. He doesn't begin to prove a case that all spoken language in all circumstances partakes of the Father's authority. He seems, however, to associate the spoken with the oratorical tradition, so that, although he is speaking in absolutes, his critique summarizes the actual social functioning of language in nineteenth-century society. This was Dickinson's society.

Derrida's attacks upon what he calls the logocentric tradition in philosophy amount to an attack upon metaphysics, especially the metaphysical signified. He notes that in traditional philosophies being is considered inseparable from presence; perhaps this connection may alert us to the possibility that Dickinson's many poems about annihilation are inevitable; once she has broken with the logocentric tradition she will also no longer be likely to see the self as presence.

In his essay 'Freud and the Scene of Writing' (*Writing and Difference*), Derrida retraces Freud's discovery of the 'trace' of the act of writing which, according to Freud, always survives in the text. Instead of the bold personal presence of the orator, we have the trace of the repressed or remembered in the text. The Freudian 'trace' may be a way of understanding how Dickinson's speaker works in her poems. The 'I' of her poems is connected with something that once happened to it, but the connection is ambiguous, expressed through the emotional colouring of the poem's metaphors, and through operations of condensation and displacement. Her 'I' is not about presence. According to Derrida, we must consider 'The repression of writing as the repression of that which threatens presence and the mastering of presence.'[16] Conversely, the foregrounding of writing in a poet like Dickinson can be said to recognize the 'trace' of the personal past without presuming 'presence'.[17]

In his conclusion, Derrida sets out a programme for future psychoanalysis in which one element would be

A *becoming-literary of the literal*. Here, despite several attempts made by Freud and certain of his successors, a psychoanalysis of literature respectful of the *originality of the literary signifier* has not yet begun, and this is surely not an accident. Until now, only the analysis of literary *signifieds*, that is, *nonliterary* signified meanings, has been undertaken. But such questions refer to the entire history of literary forms themselves . . .

(*Writing and Difference*, p. 230)

This is an incisive comment. It is curious, though, that Derrida overlooks writing itself (one might suggest Dickinson's writing in particular) as a place where the analysis of the signifier is being carried out. Dickinson, as we have seen, brings the trace forward by her linked metaphors, her interconnection of texts, and her attention to gaps and discontinuities. At the same time she protects her poetry from the limitations of biographical criticism by keeping her referents ambiguous. If we were to look at metaphors in terms of their faceting in the work of poets (rather than their non-literary 'meaning'), if poets themselves were to conceive of rich and complex metaphors without transcendence, then the history of writing would indeed change. I am saying that Emily Dickinson has already changed it.

CHAPTER FIVE

A WOMAN WRITING HERSELF

That oblique belief which we call Conjecture
Grapples with a Theme stubborn as Sublime
  ('Some we see no more, Tenements of Wonder')

Tell all the Truth but tell it slant —
Success in Circuit lies
Too bright for our infirm Delight
The Truth's superb surprise
  ('Tell all the Truth but tell it slant —')

If speech is discredited, what remains? For Dickinson, writing was a form of love; to write is a love-act, expressed throughout her poetry by language of power and ecstatic pleasure. Her metaphor-clusters of gems and crowns apply equally to writing and fulfilled love. The poet as figure is seen to grasp the word in a marital embrace: 'Shall I take thee, the Poet said/To the propounded word?'

The 'gold thread' letter began a life-long association of writing and joy. But is the joy wholly contained within the act of writing, or does Dickinson allow a written or spoken communication between people? It seems she does allow it, but only just. Several occasional poems report speech as part of some encounter, and while the speech may be charged with difficulty, it is still recognizable as discourse. Thus, in 'If He were living — dare I ask —', Dickinson dreads asking whether a dear friend is alive, lest she be informed he is dead.

Lovers or intimate friends must communicate, though in Dickinson a hierarchy of communications is maintained.

People who are close may send messages or letters which should be understood, as in the two versions of 'Going to Him! Happy letter!'. In one highly condensed poem, Dickinson admits that speech can play a role, though a limited one, in the special circumstance of love:

> Speech is one symptom of Affection
> And Silence one —

She continues, however, to prefer silence:

> The perfectest communication
> Is heard of none —

These lines support a conventional reading of love as perfect communication, but they also leave room for another reading in which the most perfect communication does not actually get 'heard' by anyone, even a lover. The second stanza supports the 'silent' reading:

> Exists and its indorsement
> Is had within —
> Behold, said the Apostle,
> Yet had not seen!

What exists? The missing grammatical subject may be 'communication' or, distantly, 'Affection', the emotion which manifests itself through opposing modes of communication. This absence is a silence, but it is a silence indicating that something exists, triggering off the poem's meditation. 'Endorsement', a term from law and commerce, means that a document is validated by one's signature on the back. The word is usually spelled with an 'e' but, as Dickinson spells it with an 'i', the 'in' of her 'indorsement' works as part of a strategy of linguistic appropriation. That silent, inner thing which is between communication and love takes over the act of validation which lawyers and businessmen think they control.

In the last two lines, Dickinson appropriates another area of discourse for her exploration of silence. The disciple, the man who follows the true prophet, says 'Behold', without having seen what he was talking about. This is certainly another of

Dickinson's slashes at verbal false confidence, particularly as expressed in the Bible. There is also a hint that the un-mentioned thing which the disciple hasn't seen shares some particulars with Dickinson's silent thing-that-exists. If we refrain from assuming that the referent is Christ or the Father, we may come closer to the unspoken, but writable, 'it'.

Spoken language has several alternatives, rather than just one opposite. Even silence can arise from different causes. In the Master letters, Dickinson struggles desperately to imagine how she might annihilate herself to please her beloved:

I will never be noisy when you want to be still. I will be ~~glad as the~~ your best little girl – nobody else will see me, but you –
     (*Letters*, II, p. 392)

To the man, a woman like Dickinson would have to be 'noisy'. Even if she doesn't utter a word, she clearly has too much to say.

A few Dickinson poems consider the possibility of absolute, non-communicative, deathly silence. This is an imposed silence, not a chosen one. In 'I was the slightest in the House –', a poem which encourages biographical reading, Dickinson wrote:

I never spoke – unless addressed –
And then, 'twas brief and low –
I could not bear to live – aloud –
The Racket shamed me so –

Trapped into silence, Dickinson writes simply that 'I had often thought/How noteless – I could die –'. Such despair occurs infrequently in Dickinson, probably because she had dis-covered that writing could be a positive silence. She was not noteless. No matter what happened to her, she could write. To be silent was not to be silenced.

For Dickinson silence communicates the strongest emotions, because it is the trope of fullness. As Dickinson wrote in a late, possibly fragmentary quatrain:

Declaiming Waters none may dread –
But Waters that are still

Are so for that most fatal cause
In Nature – they are full –

Blake used still water as an image of stagnation: 'Expect poison
from the standing water', he wrote in one of the Proverbs of
Hell in 'The Marriage of Heaven and Hell'. Dickinson, used to
life in the magic prison of the house she called 'Chillon',
stresses water's capacity to well and flow, both in the bowl and
over its edge.

When signs are given by the body, or by its social coding in
clothes, we experience a highly communicative silence.
Dickinson used her own body as a sign, from the famous white
dress to the freckles which are her code for imperfect
humanity in many poems. All bodies display some humanity.
There is less sadism than meets the eye in Dickinson's
powerful poem,

I like a look of Agony,
Because I know it's true –
Men to not sham Convulsion
Not simulate – a Throe –

Death's terrible decoration of the dying body is 'Impossible to
feign'. The linguistic basis for Dickinson's interest in death
becomes even clearer in 'The overtakelessness of those', a
poem about those who have 'accomplished Death'.

The soul her 'Not at Home'
Inscribes upon the flesh –
And takes her fair aerial gait
Beyond the hope of touch.

Non-human language, by contrast, is innately open and
frank. There cannot be a split between the animal and what it
communicates. In a not entirely comic remark to Higginson,
Dickinson once wrote that she avoided certain people because
what they say 'embarrasses my Dog'. Her loyal Carlo is a
touchstone of the authentic in several poems.

Dickinson uses the integrity of animal language most
brilliantly in the poem which begins with the dramatic line,

'Split the Lark — and you'll find the Music'. Birdsong is a classic image for unfettered lyric expression, but Dickinson literalizes the quest for the origins of song. Changing her analogy while continuing the action of splitting open, Dickinson sees music rolled up inside the bird the way the future blossom is implicit within the bulb: 'Bulb after Bulb, in Silver rolled —'. As the living container is opened,

> Loose the Flood — you shall find it patent —
> Gush after Gush, reserved for you —
> Scarlet Experiment! Skeptic Thomas!
> Now, do you doubt that your Bird was true?

The analytic 'Scarlet Experiment' unto death of dissecting the Lark should convince the 'Skeptic Thomas' to whom the poem is addressed. The lark quite literally embodies the truth that music floods out of those who are born singers. The lark-song and the blood-flow are one, a 'passion' unto death.

The immediate provenance of Dickinson's bird with music inside is a passage in Elizabeth Barrett Browning's *Aurora Leigh*, in which her poet-heroine describes the differences between women's poetry and men's poetry:

> The music soars within the little lark,
> And the lark soars. It is not thus with men.
> We do not make our places with our strains,
> Content, while they rise, to remain behind
> Alone on earth instead of so in heaven.
> No matter. . . .
>   (III, pp. 151–6)

Barrett Browning's passage solicits pity for the feminized 'little lark', but its feminist distinction between internal womanly song and ambitious male song is unmistakable.

The unstoppable flood of blood-music forms the conclusion a hundred years later, to one of Sylvia Plath's last poems, 'Kindness'. Using body language to define her poetry, Plath writes:

The blood jet is poetry,
There is no stopping it.
You hand me two children, two roses.

Plath, like Dickinson, is addressing someone, but from a nearly opposite psychic perspective. Her poem is resisting the well-intentioned blandishment of a 'Dame Kindness' who wants to put 'poultices' on a psychic body which can only write through its wound.

Dickinson locates writing in individual words and the discovery of words, both by herself and by other writers. An avid reader all her life, she seeks out writing in books and in the idea of the poet. Individual poems receive rather less attention, except through the slanted homage of allusion. Amid Dickinson's imagery of childhood emotional starvation, words and books are food. In 'Let Us play Yesterday —', a poem about the awakening of vocation, Dickinson writes of 'Easing my famine/at my Lexicon —'. In a beautiful image, she describes her own girl-mind, not yet the lark, but about to be:

Still at the Egg-life —
Chafing the Shell —
When you troubled the Ellipse —
And the Bird fell —

Now, as an adult, she perceives herself about to be imprisoned, but unnaturally: 'Can the Lark resume the Shell —', she asks. Now that she has experienced the liberty given her by the Lexicon and by her beloved teacher, she uses her skill to let her oppressor know she has figured out His plan.

God of the Manacle
As of the Free —
Take not my Liberty
Away from Me —

In what may be a conversion of the imagery of the sacrament, she asserts, in another poem, that

> Strong Draughts of Their refreshing Minds
> To drink — enables Mine
> Through Desert or the Wilderness
> As bore it Sealed Wine —

Like a camel, which contains its own drink, Dickinson's mind can survive dry privation with its inner wine. 'How powerful the Stimulus/Of an Hermetic Mind', the poem concludes, adding yet another container-image. Being sealed, carrying hermetic secrets which operate by code, seems to be part of the poet's nourishing strength.

In a well-known poem, Dickinson describes the consumption of words:

> He ate and drank the precious Words —
> His Spirit grew robust —

Nourished by writing, he forgets personal poverty and mortality:

> He danced along the dingy Days
> And this Bequest of Wings
> Was but a Book — What Liberty
> A loosened spirit brings —

The reader whom words liberate is male, and his liberation is both easily attained and complete. Dickinson seems to have chosen a male protagonist to permit her to examine untrammelled freedom without falsifying the case. The theme of escape is mingled with fancy in another poem:

> There is no Frigate like a Book
> To take us Lands away
> Nor any Coursers like a Page
> Of prancing Poetry —

In one curious poem, 'A precious — mouldering — pleasure — 'tis —/To meet an Antique Book —', Dickinson depicts the book as a part-preserved human specimen in period costume, rather like one of Swift's Struldbruggs. With Dickinson's image of the venerable old gentleman of 'quaint opinions', a tone of antiquarian preciousness enters the poem. The role of the book-man is not, however, to make the moribund charming, but to convey life — to know and tell us what happened in the present of the past,

> When Sappho — was a living Girl —
> And Beatrice wore
> The Gown that Dante — deified —

The 'presence' of a book in the present 'is Enchantment —', in Dickinson's favoured (and usually female) imagery of witchcraft. But old books can never be completely satisfying: 'Old volumes shake their Vellum Heads/And tantalize — just so —'.

Dickinson's antiquarian interest in books sounds a little like the American pedantry which Ralph Waldo Emerson attacked so eloquently in 'The American Scholar'. As 'love of the hero corrupts into worship of his statue', he wrote, 'the book becomes noxious'.[1] In fact, Dickinson loves the historic book as container for the living knowledge it gives. The authors she hero-worships live in the present or near-present, and are women.

While Dickinson was discreet about expressing views on Emerson, who was the most influential cultural figure of her time, she did use some of the terminology of 'A precious — mouldering — pleasure — 'tis —' to make a covert comment about his role. When he visited Amherst in December 1857 to lecture on 'The Beautiful in Rural Life', he stayed at The Evergreens with Austin and Sue Dickinson, who gave a reception for him. Emily Dickinson did not attend either the lecture or the party, but Sue preserved a comment which Emily was supposed to have written about the visit: 'It must have been as if he had come from where dreams are born?' (*Letters*, III, p. 913) This phrase appears in the sixth stanza of 'A precious — mouldering — pleasure — 'tis', where it refers to the ancient book-man:

> He traverses — familiar —
> As One should come to Town —
> And tell you all your Dreams — were true —
> He lived — where Dreams were born —

The comparison between Emerson and the old book is inescapable. Emily must have offered Sue some diplomatically dreamy praise to make up for her absence at the local cultural event of the year; unfortunately her compliment has lived on as proof of her adulation of Emerson. Dickinson's praise for Emerson is genuine, but it is praise of someone very ancient, someone who is, moreover, a kind of travelling salesman of optimism. That view of Emerson was also propounded, but with far greater bitterness, by Melville in *The Confidence Man*.

Dickinson does not adopt Emerson's terminology of masculine power: hero, tyrant, genius, divinely chanting poet. For Dickinson, the poet's heroism consists of his or her written silence:

> The Martyr Poets − did not tell −
> But wrought their Pang in syllable − . . .
>
> The Martyr Painters − never spoke −
> Bequeathing − rather − to their Work −
> That when their conscious fingers cease −
> Some seek in Art − the Art of Peace −

What the poet or painter has to say goes into the work, which is the direct inscription of emotion ('Pang'), not a representation of it. This poem shifts from the past tense to the subjunctive, so that 'Their mortal fate − [might] encourage Some', and the example of the artist can mean that some [might] seek the art of finding peace in the creation of art.

If poets are silent, they still illuminate. 'The Poets light but Lamps −', Dickinson begins a highly compact, short-line poem. Developing her image into a conceit, she writes that the poets themselves 'go out' but 'the Wicks they stimulate' cause a 'vital Light' to 'inhere' [attach] to them:

> Inhere as do the Suns −
> Each Age a Lens
> Disseminating their
> Circumference −

Power in Dickinson expresses itself through a leap in range and proportion between stanzas, from oil lamp to solar systems. Then, retaining the sublime sense of a universe filled with light, she changes to an optical image as her way of bringing in history. Each different age is a lens disseminating, spreading and multiplying the 'circumference' of the poet, who is now a sun-like source of light. The angle at which the poet is seen will shift as culture changes, but the poet's illumination remains.

While the poet, as seen by Dickinson, may illuminate vast reaches of space, he or she is not seen as inspired from above. For Dickinson the muse is absent or, rather, so heavily revised into sisterliness that it is no longer objectified. Poetic strength comes from intimacy with the word and with ordinariness:

> This was a Poet — It is That
> Distills amazing sense
> From ordinary Meanings —

In a synaesthetic mingling of scent and proportion, Dickinson has poets distill

> . . . Attar so immense
>
> From the familiar species
> That perished by the Door —
> We wonder it was not Ourselves
> Arrested it — before —

By validating the humblest 'familiar species' as topic for poetry, Dickinson inevitably relates her argument to Emerson's call in 'The Poet' for a new American poetry which would not disdain to treat the ordinary. Whitman took up this challenge in *Leaves of Grass*; so did Dickinson. It is at least equally important, however, that the small, humble and domestic were considered women's topics, so that when she writes about weeks, hay, grass or ordinary flowers, Dickinson is also rescuing a 'feminized' topic for her womanly vision. When Emerson had called for the railway and the factory to become 'poetic', their previous unworthiness had been due to perceived ugliness or modernity. Dickinson addresses the railway too, in 'I like to see it lap the Miles', but her main pressure is towards not caring whether her topic is too small or too big.

Yet, as Dickinson continues 'This was a Poet −', the poet as type draws away from her:

> Of Pictures, the Discloser −
> The Poet − it is He −
> Entitles Us − by Contrast −
> To ceaseless Poverty −

In her many plays upon the trope of wealth and poverty, Dickinson has often seen poverty as a kind of wealth: in 'Your Riches − taught me − Poverty', the spiritual 'wealth' of the beloved friend teaches Dickinson's speaker to exchange her 'little Wealths' for the solace 'That there exists − a Gold −', even if she does not have it herself. In 'This was a Poet −', as the poet becomes sexed as male, his wealth seems to do nothing to alleviate a genuine poverty in 'Us'. All we can do, Dickinson concludes, is 'rob' him a little. He wouldn't miss what we take, since his 'Portion' is 'unconscious'.

But who is the poet whom Dickinson describes? In these poems the poet is either male, or the poet's sex is hidden by the neutral plural 'they'. The phrase 'martyr poets' could well refer with great aptness to the Brontë sisters and, in at least one other poem, 'I died for Beauty −', Dickinson dramatises a woman poet (Elizabeth Barrett Browning) as 'He'. Dickinson wrote a number of poems which refer to particular woman poets. Still, the retention of sexual difference for the poet *type* is striking.

Dickinson's relationship to these poets is, significantly, as reader, not as fellow-poet. When she addresses that difference explicitly, as she would in the course of her investigations, the result is an even greater distance from creativity:

> I would not paint − a picture −
> I'd rather be the One −
> Its bright impossibility
> To dwell − delicious − on −

The poem continues into a familiar attack on noisy speech, as

Dickinson compares two kinds of hot air. She 'would not talk, like Cornets −', preferring to 'be the One/Raised softly to the Ceilings −' and floated out 'Through Villages of Ether −/ Myself endued Balloon'. The tone darkens when she reaches poetry:

> Nor would I be a Poet −
> It's finer − own the Ear −
> Enamored − impotent − content −
> The License to revere . . .

By 1862, the approximate date when this was composed, Dickinson had already written about five hundred poems. Yet she could still speak of herself as someone who was not a poet. The terminology of audience is unmitigatedly feminine; adoring another, but 'impotent' oneself, content to 'revere' the (poetic) licence given to others without a hint of any desire of one's own.

The concluding stanza spells out a poetics of gender conflict:

> A privilege so awful
> What would the Dower be,
> Had I the Art to stun myself
> With Bolts of Melody!

If she had this terrible and awe-full privilege, with what bride-gift would she be offered in marriage by her father? Presumably none at all. If, however, Dickinson's power extends to making herself the bride, as it does in poems like 'Mine − by the Right of the White Election!', then perhaps the Dower is the awesome gift which she embodies. As if to cleanse the implications of being given away which 'Dower' brings in, Dickinson ends the poem by writing that if she had this art it would be an art directed at herself, exhilarating but equally possibly knocking her unconscious. The phrase 'Bolts of Melody' brilliantly condenses lyric beauty with the lightning-like power that the Dickinson lyric in fact has. But the passage is written in the subjunctive.

To write and to 'be a poet' in society may have little to do with each other. In the nineteenth century, publishing was frought with contradictions for women.[2] Writing, however, could be free, not only for Dickinson, but for countless other women writers of letters, journals and 'portfolio' verse. We do not find Dickinson writing poems which wonder if they are good enough. She is not a poet who worries in writing about problems of flow, of choice of topic or form, or about appropriateness. Her output was enormous. She has complete confidence about her relationship with the language, and sees it as part of her body ('Split the Lark — and you'll find the Music —'). In 'My Life had stood — a loaded Gun —', she is actually all writerly power and nothing else. Again and again she uses linguistic terminology as a way of structuring her perceptions of the real, as if language is at least as present and actual a phenomenon to her. Yet she feared she was not 'a poet'.

It is perhaps worth stressing once again the firmness of Dickinson's writerly resolve in the face of quite severe criticism. In 1862 Higginson had called the 'gait' (metre) of her poetry 'spasmodic', though she preferred to think of it as 'elastic'. He felt her work 'uncontrolled' and 'dark', which, if taken as an objective description of her thematics, is probably true enough. Dickinson rebutted this last criticism by noting that darkness is part of nature: 'You said "Dark". I know the Butterfly — and the Lizard — and the Orchis —. Are not these *your* Countrymen?' (*Letters*, II, p. 412). Dickinson did not change her poetic practice in the slightest as a result of Higginson's criticism; if anything, the poems of 1862–3 are more spasmodic, uncontrolled and dark than her work as a whole. Instead, criticism from a sympathetic public man became part of her withdrawal from trying to publish.

But Dickinson did placate Higginson by sending him two poems that implied she was weak. The first, 'Before I got my eye put out', is a poem about both literal blindness and feminine constraint, as the blinded speaker guesses it is 'safer' within the frame of the window pane. Using the subjunctive mode to depict both past and possibility, Dickinson vividly evokes the perhaps overweening pleasure of possessing 'All Forests — Stintless Stars —', indeed the entire universe, simply by looking wherever she liked. But that was 'Before I got my put out'.[3]

In the second poem, 'I cannot dance upon my Toes', Dickinson depicts herself as unskilled because 'No Man instructed me —', a declaration which, in the larger context of her accomplishment, expresses pride rather than weakness. The poem mimics feminine humility, but then proceeds to prefer the speaker's Dionysiac 'Glee'. Precisely because she hasn't 'hopped to Audiences — like Birds,/One Claw upon the Air', she has an 'Art/I mention — easy — Here —' which is as 'full as Opera'. Dickinson's July 1862 letter to Higginson continues her play of resistance. Replying to what seems to have been an adverse comment by Higginson about pride in her poetry, Dickinson writes, 'I suppose the pride that stops the Breath, in the Core of Woods, is not of Ourself —' (*Letters*, II, p. 415). The pride is not hers but innate in the glory of what she writes about. This passage lends deeper resonance to her protestation in 'This is my letter to the World' that her 'letter' has been 'The simple News that Nature told —'.

She continues: 'You say I confess the little mistake, and omit the large — Because I can see Orthography — but the Ignorance out of sight — is my Preceptor's charge —.' She knows how to spell perfectly, thank you. The 'large' mistakes, presumably her theological unorthodoxy, she doesn't admit, but instead, with the greatest politeness, she writes that metaphysical ignorance is Higginson's problem, not hers.

In the same letter she takes on the question about whether her work is original:

I marked a line in One Verse — because I met it after I made it — and never consciously touch a paint, mixed by another person —
    I do not let go it, because it is mine.
        (*Letters*, II, p. 415)

Here she shares the romantic belief in originality, but without attention to individual genius.

Much feminist criticism comments on the woman poet having to deal with a patriarchal language. The problem is perennial. Since it has always been exacerbated historically by the denial of women's access to cultural institutions, and by patriarchal definition of what knowledge is, it can seem as if language *per se* must be patriarchal, and the woman's voice one of silence. After the Word of God and Adamic naming, where is the space for the woman's language? Dickinson experienced patriarchal control, and she did not underestimate its power. But by concentrating on the written, she separated out a resource that could be hers. By refusing to occupy the feminine space, Dickinson finds her own space in the written, away from the two false languages of social discourse and its purported authority in the reported speech of the Father. She becomes a woman who writes herself.

Amid all of Dickinson's almost sentimental love of books, there is one huge exception. This is the Bible, which she perceives as largely a repository of untruths. In her late poems, the case against a tyrant-God seemed to her to be conclusive. She wrote coldly:

> The Bible is an antique Volume
> Written by faded Men.
> At the suggestion of Holy Spectres —

No antiquarian charm here. But her distancing of the received vocabulary of belief goes back early, probably to the period of her adolescent religious doubt. In an inversion of the Christian view of pagan myth, Dickinson often represents the Bible as a survival from an early human era. In 'Better — than Music! For I — who heard it —', Eden is 'a legend — dimly told'. This sentiment occurs in several other poems.

In the late 1850s, when Dickinson began to write her earlier surviving poems, she underlined many words to emphasize their ambiguity. She put other words in inverted commas to set them off, often ironically, and she directed attention to significant individual words by capitalizing them. As her work developed in the early 1860s, she kept the emphatic capitalization and used syntactic distortion and ellipses to create her characteristic broken rhetoric. When she wrote about the Bible, however, she continued to use inverted commas, a habit which also makes it the book she quotes most often directly.

Other allusions, such as those to Shakespeare or Elizabeth Barrett Browning, are melded with her own text. It is as if she is not admitting the Word of God into her poem, but must address it just the same, because she must address issues raised by its presence.

The instances of Dickinson's sceptical citation are so numerous that I shall only give some. In the early poem 'Houses' — so the Wise Men tell me —' she quotes Jesus when she mentions the 'Many Mansions' she has been told the Father built, 'In my Father's House there are many mansions' (John 14:2). Then she adds in the same breath, '*I* don't know him'. Many of Dickinson's sceptical poems are structured as replies to a false or unprovable Biblical assertion. One begins, 'You're right — "the way is narrow" ', seeming to agree with Matthew 7:14, only to sabotage the argument later. ' "Red Sea", indeed!' she begins another affronted reply: 'Talk not to me/Of purple Pharaoh —'. 'And with what body do they come?' — she begins a poem of hope, quoting St Paul's First Epistle to the Corinthians. Only if the dead can truly live again in body will they be 'real' and she can 'know that it is them!'

Dickinson uses inverted commas to frame words whose received meaning she is questioning. ' "Morning" — means "Milking" — to the Farmer —', she begins one poem, the point being that morning means much more than the daily repetition of duty. These framed inadequate usages cluster around the terminology of the Father. 'What is — "Paradise" —' she begins a series of ironically wishful queries in an early poem. The child mode is useful here; children can ask anything. '"Heaven" — is what I cannot reach!' Dickinson begins a poem of loss. And, in a happier association of the unknowable metaphysical with the sensuous physical, '"Heaven" has different Signs — to me —' begins a list of luscious places which 'remind us of the place/That Men call "Paradise" —'. Dickinson puts the Father in quotation marks, too: '"Heavenly Father" — take to thee' asks the Father to accept sinful, iniquitous humanity, even though it would be more respectful if the Father would trust the human instead.

'"Faith" is a fine invention', she begins an early four-line poem, as if faith were a mechanical contraption. However, the poem concludes, she prefers her own finely tuned '*Microscopes* . . . In an Emergency'. Even the famous definition-poem, ' "Hope" is the thing with feathers —' offsets 'Hope' so that its meaning can be redefined rather than merely repeated. Throughout these bracketings, Dickinson finds the Bible acting as voice of the Father. In a few poems she hopes she may be mistaken, but in most, particularly her later poems, she is in no doubt that the negative, denying, tyrannical face of the Bible accurately represents the nature of its divine author. '"Heavenly Father" — take to thee' concludes with a bitter attack upon the Father, supposedly 'candid', who has none-theless created man sinful:

> — 'We are Dust' —
> We apologize to thee
> For thine own Duplicity —

In her own comment on duplicity, Dickinson has buried a latinate antithesis in 'candid', which means 'white' in Latin. This white God who embodies truth is actually duplicitous, the way primary words can be. Dickinson does not forgive God; she ironically apologises to Him for what He has done to humanity, since He appears unable to apologize to us.

What Dickinson's society thought of as its centre, namely agreed social discourse, was closed to her, partly by choice, partly by the conventions imposed by social gendering. Nonetheless, her urge to experience and know expressed itself in language. Indeed, as in modern poetry, Dickinson's questions get formulated only within language, through linguistic acts which occur on what she calls her 'circumference', the written. Literary language easily becomes clogged by out-moded conventions. It feels too ornamental, distanced from the vividness and accuracy of everyday speech, the way Victorian poetry felt by the turn of the century. Dickinson's poetry avoids this limitation because she doesn't write in 'poetic diction'; she doesn't use a specified, traditional language which defines what is written in it as 'literature'. Yet her condensed, syntactically broken writing does not take its model from speech either.

Despite the vehemence with which modern poets such as Pound and Eliot attacked Victorian poetic diction, Dickinson may help us to see that the written itself isn't the enemy. The moderns were, in fact, very strongly drawn to modes of writing which cannot be reduced to speech. The ideogram, pictograph and hieroglyph all tend towards the cryptogram, the decodable visual sign, not towards the verbal (or at least this is how the moderns chose to understand them). Modern attention to the shape of the poem on the page also shows a bias towards the written. If Dickinson's inscribed language is given an historical place, this 'written' aspect of modernism can also receive a more just appraisal.

Perhaps future generations can reclaim spoken language from the authority claimed by the Logos. But that is not the assignment Dickinson gave herself. While cutting off poetry from social discourse must create problems in the long term, it can be a source of tremendous strength for the individual poet. Indeed, it may *only* be in writing that the power of the Logos can be circumvented. Because of the historic association of poetry with speech, there has been little literary criticism of this subject. Derrida, who does address the issue, keeps away from the person who writes.

Some of the most perceptive discussions of the way the written relates to the mind are found in essays by Freud. Any feminist critic must address Freud with great scepticism, since his elevation of the gender terms 'masculine' and 'feminine' into absolutes has caused untold harm. Nonetheless, his meditations on the written illuminate Dickinson's accomplishment and point to some huge consequences it may have.

Freud's release from seeing writing as a merely mechanical adjunct to memory came when he realized that dreams and memory traces (conscious and unconscious) were themselves a kind of writing, an inscription, even though 'psychic writing' has no text. In a 1910 essay, 'The Antithetical Meaning of Primary Words', Freud was most definite that dreams were writing. In this passage, 'language', a translation of the German

'Sprache', is being used to mean both spoken language and language in general:

> It seems to us more appropriate to compare dreams with a system of writing than with language. In fact, the interpretation of a dream is completely analogous to the decipherment of an ancient pictographic script such as Egyptian hieroglyphics. In both cases there are certain elements which are not intended to be interpreted (or read, as the case may be) but are only designed to serve as 'determinatives', that is to establish the meaning of some other element.[4]

So instead of writing being a transcription or translation of the authentic event, there are two kinds of writing, psychic writing and text writing.

In the passage from 'The Antithetical Meaning of Primary Words', Freud stresses the importance of 'determinatives' or 'link' elements, just as Dickinson does when she constructs her diadems of meaning. At least with some terms, the meaning is not found outside or beyond, but generated in the circumference of associations. Spoken language has no reliable relation to inner history, since it is not fixed, materialized by inscription. Our current conversational description of, say, our mother, or of a curious dream about a house, will be different from what it would have been ten years ago. New memories have been laid down, the old ones have been condensed or shifted. Since personal presence is part of speech, we are likely to perform a little in conversation, and to trim our description to have the desired effect on our audience. We, the fixed person, get in the way of our own traces. The link we are making is between ourselves and society.

If Freud is right and the written does have a particularly intimate similarity to psychic 'work', then it will always be written language which will be the closer to the mind. The poet who, like Dickinson, installs the trace at the centre of her poetics will be closest of all.[5] Freud's analogy between mind and writing may be taken even further. In the mid-1920s, Freud became intrigued by a children's writing apparatus known as the Mystic Writing Pad. These pads, which are still available, consist of a wax backing covered with a paper sheet which is protected by a strip of celluloid. When you press on the paper with a stick or your fingernail, 'writing' appears. When you lift the paper and celluloid, the writing disappears, though its trace remains on the wax beneath. Freud felt that this device perfectly represented the way the mind 'writes' since, after a certain point, for new images to be inscribed, old ones must be erased. They are never erased completely, though, since their trace always remains inscribed beneath the new inscription.

Freud doesn't extend his speculation further, and he doesn't notice that writing does change after it is written down, because its readers change. Also, like Derrida in his essay 'Freud and the Scene of Writing' (*Writing and Difference*), Freud doesn't look in poetry for evolved uses of the trace. There are certainly homages to the trace in modern art.[6] If, however, we turn the analogy of the Mystic Writing Pad in the direction of Dickinson's poetry, her psychological accuracy is enhanced still further. Her curious mixture of care for language of the poem and apparent carelessness for its long-term future may itself be a message about the appropriate status of a text which is trying to come as close as possible to the way the mind investigates. As she rewrote her poems, many became a kind of collage of traces.[7] In 'Publication – is the Auction', her final riposte to the literary market-place was that rather than publish, she would return white unto her white creator – she would die unwritten upon by the Logos. She would also rather be erased than 'invest – Our Snow'. Snow-writing has its time, and then melts. Snow as type comes again next year. As so often in Dickinson, something which may have been forced on her became an agency for discovering a truth.

The confluence of the written and the womanly in Dickinson has immense historical implications. Dickinson's validation of the written offers us that 'written' in its first flowering as womanly writing. That womanliness is highly appropriate – it may even be necessary – since only those who are outside the temptations of the Logos are free to create their own method of inscription.

CHAPTER SIX

THE HOUSE WITHOUT THE DOOR

In my Father's house are many mansions: if it were not so, I would have told you.
  (John, 14:2)

'Many Mansions', by 'his Father',
I don't know him; snugly built!
Could the Children find the way there –
Some, would even trudge tonight!
  ('"Houses" – so the Wise Men tell me –')

Doom is the House without the Door –
'Tis entered from the Sun –
And then the Ladder's thrown away,
Because Escape – is done –
  ('Doom is the House without the Door –')

The 'house' was a highly charged place for Emily Dickinson, as, to some extent, it is for all of us. There seem, however, to have been certain factors which made the house particularly important for her poetry. First is the biographical fact that Dickinson lived all of her life, except for a fifteen-year interval, in the same house, and that house was run to serve her father. Dickinson's poetry is a kind of test case for the presence the house of the father can have in the writing of the daughter. Dickinson had a pragmatic imagination; the Homestead was the central 'given' out of which she worked. The Homestead was also an over-determined place, carrying a heavy burden of other people's desires and projections, even before Dickinson wrote a word about it. Her poetry takes account of that turmoil.

In different Dickinson poems and letters the 'house' she lives in is variously her heritage, her father, palace, citadel, mausoleum, coffin, museum, library, place of literary production, inner sanctum, refuge when in flight, place of duty, prison, and place of starvation where food may be served, but not to Emily. This is what the house *is*, for the purpose of a given poetic investigation; it is not sometimes 'like' a prison while still remaining objectively itself.

What the Dickinson house is *not* is equally significant: not a ruin, despite its links with the past, not a nursery, not a place of nourishment, not warm or a hearth, not a place of family love, society or celebration. All of these facets have been structured by Dickinson; they are what she made of the house. Some contradict her practice in life. For example, she was an accomplished baker, both of bread and cakes, and she enjoyed giving her produce to friends. She gave cakes, flowers and poems, separately and together. She often uses imagery of food in her poetry, but not in connection with the house. Also, despite being a citadel of sorts, the house of the father offers little protection. It is easily invaded by death, objects of fear, or the gaze and acts of others. These can enter by window, latch or door, or appear already installed as troubling co-inhabitants, like the phallic 'Worm' in the dream-poem 'In Winter in my Room'.

The Jungian term 'imago' might describe the complex of uses Dickinson makes of the house, were it not that 'imago' tends to mean a neurotic, usually stereotypical construct, something imposed upon the object. Dickinson's 'house' is not an unconscious distorting 'set' through which she must try to see the real place where she lives. Indeed, much of the difficulty surrounding Dickinson's house imagery arises from her struggle *not* to depict the 'imaginary' house, a house which is always resembling something in a mentality in which all ideas of resemblance originate in the mirror image of oneself.

The house is one of those signifying images, like gem or sea or bird, which Dickinson analyses, breaking it open and exposing its different facets in the course of her investigation. The house, however, doesn't seem always to have been sufficiently open or 'known' for Dickinson to use it regularly as an epistemological tool. Dickinson does appear to 'know' the figures of the father, mother, sister or self, even though these figures would seem to be at least as difficult to encounter as the image of the house. Her patriarchal analysis has a conclusive feel. For Dickinson, the house is a deeply ambiguous image whose ambiguity remains unresolved. Looking at the house image yields information about how Dickinson dealt with areas which she could not command. The house is part of the poetic subject while also being an object (both literally and figuratively). It is inside her while she is inside it.

In a number of Dickinson poems about houses she seems not to have made up her mind what the house means, and reference to other poems only points up more ambiguity. In still others references to houses seem to have been brought in where they do not seem strictly necessary. Instead of the house being part of a linked cluster of meanings, it expresses opposites. While its appearance as image or metaphor can have a gem-like clarity, more often the rest of the poem is circling round the ambiguity which has been provoked by the house.

Such issues are not accidental. Since being in her father's house was a circumstance Dickinson considered beyond her control, the house is the most apt image possible (except perhaps the body) for writing about the borderline between inner and outer, between what one has generated and what is given, between present and past. It is probably a richer image than the body for these issues since the body, not being cultural, is not an apt measure for the influence of the past, and it can also encourage an easy dualism. For Dickinson the house also enables these borderline areas to be treated without issues of convention and social discourse constantly raising their head. 'Home' occupies a slightly different part of Dickinson's figurative range, tending to be the final home, whether heaven or tomb.

The objective presence of the house makes it another of Dickinson's metonyms; what houses generate is another way of writing about actual houses. Dickinson seems to have wanted to avoid seeing where she lived or her self as part of a world of resemblance, but she also didn't wish to fall into the contrary error of assuming either her immediate setting or self to be 'beyond' language. She uses the house to press very hard on this linguistic and philosophic issue, until it is possible to see her working out a highly innovative poetics of container and contained. Since at the same time she cannot ignore the father's control over what is also hers, the house image often carries an emotional weight of stress and pain.

The ambiguous object-status of the house raises another issue which Dickinson addresses when she writes about houses. This is whether the body of the father can occupy a position for the daughter comparable to that which the body of the mother occupies for the son. Does the father have a body, or is he only his name? In the absence of an adequate literary or psycho-analytic theoretical literature on the father's body, the daughter's mind, and their consequences for representation, when Dickinson addresses herself to such issues she is writing, as she so often does, at the limits of our knowledge as well as of her own.

In general, sometimes conventional terms, Dickinson can represent qualities of consciousness, heart, body and person by the metaphor of the house. In one of the many affectionate letters she wrote to Samuel Bowles in 1862–3, she wrote,

How sweet it must be to one to come Home – whose Home is in so many Houses – and every Heart a 'Best Room'. I mean you, Mr Bowles.

(*Letters*, II, p. 416)

One of those homes is Emily's heart. So the house is not always a signified; it also is a signifier for other meanings. This reversible semiological function indicates the house's non-meta-physical status. It also indicates the proximity of the house image to some conjunction between signifier and signified, in which case no knowledge can be mined from the image.

A house can be seen most clearly when it is being looked at or when it is being looked out of, so that it is what frames and determines what is seen. Dickinson doesn't look at her house as entity. There are no poems in which the house she lives in is an entire object which is first described and then interpreted. Nor are there surviving descriptive letters. We don't get Dickinson the character looking at, or considering the house she lives in. Dickinson doesn't seem to want to involve the house in representation, perhaps because she might find it inaccurate to 'see it clearly'. Clarity occurs at a distance, as in the lovely nocturnal tale 'I know some lonely Houses off the Road'.

Dickinson wrote many poems about looking out of her house, seeing other houses, trees, the road, passers-by, callers, and those who do not stop to call. These poems take on great immediacy in the light of her situation, as she sat at her window in the Homestead. The plaintive poem 'I could die — to know —' depicts a shut-in Emily looking out at everyday village business: 'News-Boys salute the Door —' and 'Morning's bold face — stares in the window —' watching her and mocking the supposed privacy of the house. The speaker remarks that 'While I — dream — Here', fixed in place and fantasizing, the more important life of her lover has been proceeding elsewhere. 'To the very Square — His foot is passing — Possibly, this moment —'. Although its use of the house as prison and fortress is characteristic of Dickinson, this poem is unusual for her work in having a personal speaker writing throughout from a perspective fixed in a specific time and place. It is an occasional poem; it interests itself in action which is out of sight but nonetheless genuinely occurring. In cinematic terms, it concerns itself with events out of frame. The speaker longs for what the poem has decided she cannot see. This perspective of absence is not dissimilar to the full-blown male poetic portrait of the lovelorn woman, like Tennyson's plaintive, passive heroine in 'Mariana'. Mariana is trapped in her ruined house and can only utter obsessively repetitious variations on 'My life is dreary/He cometh not'. Lacking the phallus, the woman can only express lack. Dickinson generally analyses loss rather than reproducing its conditions; the structuring of female emotion may indicate that she is writing in relation to a formidable obstacle when she writes about, or out of, the house.

Dickinson's pragmatic imagination usually centres her poem on the question or issue that is before it. Specific incident, sight or even person serve as kinds of pre-poetic energy. Their trace may remain in the poem's intensity of mediation, even if the reference has been left in the silence before the poem. 'The Wind begun to knead the Grass' is, strictly speaking, a poem of landscape description, conventional enough for Dickinson to have sent it out twice, first to Higginson and then, in 1883, to Thomas Niles, a Boston publisher who had expressed interest in her work. The poem exists in two versions, with the version that was sent out having more conventional imagery and punctuation. Both versions offer a complex display of gender in relation to perspective and possession of the place from which the poem comes.

The house of the father is not visible in 'The Wind begun to knead the Grass' until the end, but it has been framing the poem all along. In the first version,

> The Wind begun to knead the Grass —
> As Women do a Dough —
> He flung a Hand full at the Plain —
> A Hand full at the Sky —

The female domestic imagery has been separated from the House itself, as well as from incident. We do not see Emily in the kitchen kneading dough and noticing that a storm is brewing. Such kneading, being part of Dickinson's knowledge of plasticity, is used to indicate both the storm's power and the thickness of the air while keeping the imagery of the heavens emphatically material. Nor is Dickinson simply feminizing to make the heavens more like her; if the action is gendered female, the agent is male: 'He flung'.

Domestic imagery is part of the Puritan poetic heritage, being found in emblem poems and in such poems as Edward Taylor's 'Huswifery', in which the poet asks his Lord to make him 'thy Spinning Wheele compleate', so that he may be clothed in 'Holy Robes for glory', by a God whose actions are in this case gendered female. In Puritan discourse, domestic imagery shows how the Word of God is made manifest in even the most humble actions and objects. In Dickinson the domestic image offers a material figuration for an action of air; hers is a metaphor of descent.

In the second version,

> The Wind begun to rock the Grass
> With threatening Tunes and low —
> He threw a Menace at the Earth —
> A Menace at the Sky.

The female action of kneading has been altered to a musical image whose gendering is both less explicit and, because of its lack of stress, more threatening. The wind is rocking the grass like a sinister mother, except that it is not a mother, but a thundering Jupiterean male who throws, not a thunderbolt, but its abstract metonymy, a 'Menace', at the earth. Here, as in the imagery of kneaded air, the signified is again more concrete than its signifier.

Throughout the middle range of air, Dickinson engages in a play of proportions, one of her ways of manipulating power without denying its existence. The sky is cradle or dough, the road shrinks, and a huge bird fills the sky. Animals flee to their pathetic shelters as the storm worsens. The imagery is titanic, but not Christian. Then, in the climax this attack of nature upon itself,

> The Waters Wrecked the Sky —
> But overlooked my Father's House —
> Just Quartering a Tree —

Except for punctuation, both versions conclude the same. This rush of power passes over the solid house of the father. The house has been providing the psychological perspective for the poem, and to some extent a visual perspective as well; since the storm is seen and heard but not felt or scented, Dickinson must be inside the house. While it is far too vivid to be mere explanation, the poem resembles contemporary descriptive poems about topics accepted as inherently poetic. Emerson criticized this limitation in his essay 'The Poet', but he practised it himself in poems like 'The Snow-Storm' and 'The

Rhodora'. Dickinson is indeed writing from inside the house of the father, both personally and culturally.

In 'By my Window have I for scenery', another poem set in the frame of a window, Dickinson begins at a window of her father's house and proceeds exuberantly outwards. The poem explores the mutually superimposed images of pine tree and sea in a manner that anticipates H.D.'s Imagist classic 'Oread'.

> By my Window have I for Scenery
> Just a Sea — with a Stem —
> If the Bird and the Farmer — deem it a 'Pine' —
> The Opinion will serve — for them —

As in many other poems, Dickinson claims her right to re-name what she writes about, with the mock-deprecatory 'just' calling attention to her daring. The 'scenery' framed by the window refuses to stay in perspective or proportion. Its detail is arrived at through a teasing out of the implications of the initial conceit, which provides the metaphoric base for the first half of the poem. In the next quatrain this sea is said to have no 'Line', no equator, while a squirrel has a 'giddy Peninsula'. Translated to a framed picture, the 'Line' would be a horizon-line, and the peninsula is presumably a waving branch. However, the image isn't explained. The signifier flies free, unexplained, elaborating the tree-sea metaphor as if it were actually an ocean which was being looked at. Such elaboration resembles the practice of the emblem poem, except that what the doubled tree-sea image might emblematize isn't present; rather, tree is sea, which is tree.

Dickinson travels through the senses of sight, taste, smell ('Spice — I infer from Odors borne'), hearing and proportion, or proportion-play, a perceptual mode which appears often in her work as her challenging replacement for perspectival sight. The poem shifts suddenly into a meditation upon the visible and invisible, using the rhetorical question 'Can the Dumb — define the Divine?' as transition. Dumb things *can* define divinity, when their muteness makes the sound of the Aeolean harp, singing from force of wind. Here, melody is partaking in

an undoing of language, an act whch is beautifully expressed
by language:

> The Definition of Melody – is –
> That Definition is none –
>
> It – suggests to our Faith –
> They – suggest to our Sight –

'They' would seem to be the dumb pines, though the shift
from singular to plural is troubling. From melody and sugges-
tion Dickinson moves directly to the assertion that when sight
'is put away' she 'shall meet with Conviction' that 'Immortal-
ity' which she 'somewhere met' already. The poem ends with a
metaphysical speculation, reinforced by an allusion, perhaps to
Fellows of the Royal Society:

> Was the Pine at my Window a 'Fellow
> Of the Royal' Infinity?
> Apprehensions – are God's introductions –
> To be hallowed – accordingly –

Back in the Christian perspective, the pine is a pine; Dickinson
now agrees with the bird and the farmer. Any sense of extra
meaning has been given it by God, who is the transcendent signified towards which all meaning in nature tends.
Transcendent presence would seem to silence the kind of
non-metaphysical metaphor of knowledge that plays with
proportion and takes pleasure in nature. The question about
the pine's membership of an élite group can't be answered,
only respected. In epistemological terms, the poem ends back
before when it began.

It may be well to recall at this point another poem:

> Delight – becomes pictorial –
> When viewed through Pain –
> More fair – because impossible
> That any gain –

The fixed 'pictorial' perspective is one of suffering. Any 'view'
is framed; the window of pain makes pleasure such a framed

view. The beautiful is seen to be most beautiful when it is not part of any relationship, not subject to any contract, outside of the economy of 'gain'. The mountain isn't giving a compensatory delight to an otherwise unhappy viewer; it *is* delight, in a Bunyanesque metonym. Dickinson doesn't judge this state; she analyses it, finding in 'view' something like what Freud called scopic drive, the drive towards visual pleasure. Dickinson assiduously separates her pleasure from any drive to possess, or devour what is seen. Her look is not the male gaze which Freud so closely associated with sadism in his essay 'Instincts and their Vicissitudes'.

When viewed pictorially, the mountain cannot respond:

> The Mountain − at a given distance −
> In Amber − lies −
> Approached − the Amber flits − a little −
> And That's − the Skies −

Dickinson knows well that the 'other' isn't to be known; she presumes no motive for its mountainness, its quiddity. When it is looked at again, closer up, the shift in perspective yields a definition rather than a metaphor; that flitting amber is merely the skies, just as the 'sea' outside the window was merely a pine after all. A step closer still leaves the object as a thing in a frame.

In Dickinson's many object-poems, she sends her gaze inside the single bird, flower, weed or animal she has chosen; in these close-focus poems no question of frame arises. She wrote fewer poems of landscape, perceiving that these came closer to the field then claimed by art. Though she seems to have followed her father in favouring American expansionism at the time of the Mexican War, she doesn't share the literary imperialism which sees the North American continent (or the seas) as a wilderness to be conquered.[1] The imperial sublime of Thomas Cole's 'Westward the Course of Empire' series of paintings, in which magnificent scenery creates a large-scale symbolic effect, is quite alien to Dickinson.[2] Even when Dickinson evokes her own garden, her patch of her father's estate, she doesn't possess it. Yet for Dickinson − as sometimes for Thoreau −

this is a position to be desired. Her freedom and pleasure are expressed through a riot of mixed perspectives and mingled senses.

In 'The Trees like tassels — hit — and swung —', the trees wave, insects sing 'far Psalteries of Summer', the sun came and went, different birds sat or gossiped, the snake had his 'silver matters' to attend to. Then, in a beautiful play of proportion, the climax pulls the sublime into the specific, unique life of one blossom:

Bright Flowers slit a Calyx
And soared upon a Stem
Like Hindered Flags — Sweet hoisted —
With Spices — in the Hem —

The delicious half-satisfaction of nature's complex life seems to be experienced from inside and outside at once, so that what is happening in nature is perfectly matched to the random wandering of our senses and thoughts. Dickinson does not consider writing to be in conflict with nature, but she does criticize art for failing to get inside the images it portrays. In 'How the old Mountains drip with Sunset', Guido Reni, Titian and Domeniarino are all failures.

In her conclusion Dickinson cannot resist pointing the lesson that this polymorphous wealth is considered poverty by those who choose to see nature in frames:

'Twas more — I cannot mention —
How mean — to those that see —
Vandyke's Delineation
Of Nature's — Summer Day!

In Emily Dickinson's poetry there are houses from which no one emerges. These are houses without windows or doors, except perhaps a slot in the top to lower the victim through. They are tombs and prisons, or combinations of the two in an uncanny, deathly womb. Dickinson's resistance to the power of the father is most successful when she turns this imagery of the cruel container against him. In one of her finest poems, 'Safe in their Alabaster Chambers', there is no speaker accusing the patriarchs; the poem creates its own authority through its terrible imagery:

> Safe in their Alabaster Chambers —
> Untouched by Morning —
> And untouched by Noon —
> Lie the meek members of the Resurrection —
> Rafter of Satin — and Roof of Stone!

Every detail has been considered. Alabaster is a white veined soapstone; softer than marble, it is translucent when sliced thinly. Chambers are not only rooms, they are the professional term for lawyers' offices. The members of the Resurrection are the Puritan élite, who hypocritically require luxury even in the tomb.

'Safe in their Alabaster Chambers' exists in two versions, one thought to be from 1859, and another from 1861. In the earlier version, the élite 'sleep' in their tomb. Sleep, a euphemism for death, also implies the ability to dream. In the early version, the alternative to the tomb-container is happy nature:

> Light laughs the breeze
> In her Castle above them,
> Babbles the Bee in a stolid Ear,
> Pipe the Sweet Birds in ignorant cadence, —
> Ah, what sagacity perished here!

'Ignorant cadence' and 'stolid' have the Dickinson ring, but otherwise nature is behaving in clichés.

Dickinson's passage is in fact startlingly similar to a stanza in 'The House of Death' (first book publication 1877), one of the best known poems of Louise Chandler Moulton (1835–1908), a conventional American poet whose work was well regarded in her lifetime.[3] Moulton wrote that around the house where a lovely woman has died

> The birds make insolent music
>   Where the sunshine riots outside;
> And the winds are merry and wanton,
>   With the summer's pomp and pride.

When Sue Dickinson criticized Emily's second stanza about nature, she wrote a different one: 'Perhaps this verse would please you better — Sue —'. It didn't please Sue any better: 'I am not suited dear Emily with the second verse —' (*Letters*, II, p. 379). It did seem to please Emily Dickinson, though, because 'Safe in their Alabaster Chambers' was one of the four poems she sent to Higginson with her first letter.

In the revised second stanza, it is not nature, but her poetry's power to play with proportion that shows up the grotesque pretensions of the élite:

> Grand go the Years — in the Crescent — above them —
> Worlds scoop their Arcs —
> And Firmaments — row —
> Diadems — drop — and Doges — surrender —
> Soundless as dots — on a Disc of Snow —

Dickinson, usually so drawn to the singular, pluralizes even the firmament. She is making her 'circumference' the entire universe. The Doge surrendered once, when Venice fell to Napoleon, but for Dickinson here, all history shrinks to repetitions. The heavens curve and swoop like time's scythe, except that they are utterly beyond human time. She writes these lines without a fixed visual perspective, in an agnostic sublime that sees time and space as one. The poem's last line is one of Dickinson's most compelling and far-fetched images. 'Soundless' emphasizes the absence of sound; 'dots — on a Disc of Snow' also evokes absence, perhaps throughout the entire universe. Yet the source of this eerie power is elusive. Black specks on white are the inverse of white stars on black in the night sky. They are also an image of something soiled, possibly the immaculate purity of non-existence as it is flecked by the planets on which even smaller specks live. Snow eventually melts, so even this deathly image is part of some incalculably huge movement towards the end of the universe. The end is innate in the material; there's no apocalypse. The disc is flat, with nothing beyond it. Although — perhaps *because* — 'Safe in their Alabaster Chambers' is one of the most uncompromising poems about death in our language, it displays a certain cold joy. To write and see out of frame — to fly out of the tomb of the Fathers — does give pleasure, even if it must be the pleasure of knowing and writing the black ways of the universe.

There are also tombs for the living in Dickinson. In these she does not escape the law of the Father. The prison-house is an inheritance of blank walls, a repository for the silenced. Inside this house, time seems to have stopped. Meanwhile time continues, until its passage makes the prisoner come to love the only place where she is truly at home. In early 1862 Dickinson wrote to Samuel Bowles, 'If I amaze[d] your kindness — My Love is my only apology. To the people of "Chillon" — this — is enoug[h] — I have met — no othe[rs]' (*Letters*, II, p. 393). In a typically condensed allusion, Dickinson refers to Byron's poem 'The Prisoner of Chillon' (1816). Comforted by the free song of a bird, François de Bonnivard survives, but when he is finally released, he leaves his prison unwillingly, having grown used to his chains. Time passing makes imprisonment the normal state for Byron's hero. The imprisoned Dickinson speaker suffers the same fate. 'A Prison gets to be a friend —' she begins one poem. Gradually the 'Demurer Circuit' — here gender-coded — reduces pleasure to 'A Geometric Joy' until 'this Phantasm Steel' expands to make its closed round pass for life itself.

'They shut me up in Prose' one of Dickinson's most powerful poems of imprisonment, offers itself up to biographical speculation:

> They shut me up in Prose —
> As when a little Girl
> They put me in the Closet —
> Because they liked me 'still' —

The homely sadism of the opening quatrain locates the pain in the person; 'me' approaches Emily. 'They', the unnameable and apparently all-powerful authorities, seek to 'shut up' the 'me': coffin-like enclosure, passivity and silence interlock, with the false speech of 'prose' the current preferred locking device ('shut' being both a past and present tense). She is inside a box inside a box; if this is a screen-image for herself inside the womb, it is a womb without warmth or potentiality for birth.

She asks whether adulthood will continue the constrained silence of the imprisoned child. Dickinson's child is not seen to experience or figure forth the 'clouds of glory' which Words-worth attributes to the child and to which Dickinson seems to allude in those poems in which she seeks to escape punishment by pretending to be a child. 'They shut me up in Prose —' is both an account of childhood and of the denial of adulthood. As such it stands with William Blake's adolescent lyric 'How Sweet I Roam'd from Field to Field', which uses a bird image and similar rhetorical strategies to define an opposing dynamic. Blake locates the springs of poetic expression in the sexual en-slavement that begins with puberty. Dickinson sees sexual fulfil-ment and the freedom of writing as two kinds of liberation.

Dickinson boldly declares herself free, but at the high price of dualism:

> Still! Could themself have peeped —
> And seen my Brain — go round —
> They might as wise have lodged a Bird
> For Treason — in the Pound —

'They' have committed a category mistake. Dickinson's bird, like the imagination, lives beyond good and evil. Its purported 'treason' is a projection of the jailor's jealousy of its freedom; and, in any case, the pound is for dogs. Significantly, although Dickinson elsewhere personifies birds as female, this bird is male, unlike the little girl whose imagination it represents:

> Himself has but to will
> And easy as a Star
> Abolish his Captivity —
> And laugh — no more have I —

Dickinson's bird-speaker, not consistently mythologized, connects freedom with mature song and does not allow that one can exist without the other.

The boldness of Dickinson's claim makes hard work for that part of the 'I' which is the person. From star back through bird to mind and potentially to the shut-in girl is a long journey, attested to syntactically by the double ellipses: 'Himself has but to will' (He need do no more than will) and 'No more have I' (I also do not need to do anything but will). Also the bird and 'they' are both described as having 'self', while the 'I' does not receive this referent.

Dickinson's metaphor for mind has been able to prove freedom by sheer declaration, both in the poem's assertion and in its metaphoric language when it 'abolishes' imprisonment by verbal fiat.[4] It is much less certain whether it can pull the person along with it. The literal meaning of 'No more have I' — namely, 'I have no more' — is not entirely suppressed. The poem ends with an ambiguous veering towards limits, perhaps necessarily, since to separate mind from body is to undergo an experience of death.

Often, what Dickinson saw framed by her window was indeed death, which, like the sun, enters where it pleases. 'There's been a Death, in the Opposite House' Dickinson wrote, seeing how a mattress, not a seed, appears in the opened 'pod' of the opposite window as 'somebody flings' it out to air.

A Window opens like a Pod —
Abrupt — mechanically —

Somebody flings a Mattress out —
The Children hurry by —
They wonder if it died — on that —
I used to — when a Boy —

The mattress, a metonym of the corpse that lay on it, rouses superstitious dread of what is known to exist but is hidden from sight by the limited perspective of the viewer. Dread of that which is out of frame is the central situation of gothic; what is to the side may also be what is below, beneath consciousness.

This pod-container carries the seed of death, not life. A house opposite is a mirror reflection of one's own house, its image an imaginary representation of one's own circumstance. Dickinson both blocks and accepts this reflection by her gender shift; the present-tense speaker is a man who, when a little boy, used to make his way into the house of death. Awed curiosity about death is not gender-specific. Why, then, a male speaker? Whoever that speaker is, if he is male, he is by definition not-I, not Emily Dickinson. The first person speaker is an 'other', not a persona in the sense of a mask of the self so much as an effort to make a mask which will look as if it is hiding the features of someone else. By this magic of changed gender, the reflection opposite won't be able to return to the originating house, the Homestead. 'His' house, from which the male speaker is looking out, may also be possessed by him in a way that Dickinson's house can never be possessed by her. Perhaps a man can look out upon resemblance, even in the horrific present of its unfolding, and say confidently, 'I know' what it means, while 'she' may not; perhaps she *should not* claim immediate knowledge when, as we know, the house from which she would look is not hers.

Neighbours 'rustle in and out' of the house opposite. The minister, the milliner, little boys, and the 'Man/Of the Appalling Trade' all boldly enter into the house which had once been a private place; the undertaker will soon enter the body of the deceased. Their intrusion has been justified by the deeper invasion of death. The message of power, of the gutting of the house, is clear. Entered by death, the house is uncannily 'numb', its actions 'mechanical', as if it has crossed a border-line from human to machine. Dickinson's speaker remarks,

> It's easy as a Sign —
> The Intuition of the News —
> In just a Country Town —

Reading death is easy; the sign interprets itself.

When power is available, Dickinson's speaker shoots out of the house to play in the garden or the universe; she abolishes the prison that others have made for her. When power is not available, when she feels weak, childlike, or like the economic dependent she actually was, Dickinson knows well that there are only two routes out of the House of the Father, and both lead to other men's residences. The woman may marry, or she may die and be carried to her tomb. In one of her saddest poems, 'Her Sweet turn to leave the Homestead', Dickinson mingles imagery of the bride and the corpse. The 'darker' way of departure leads to the grave. The metonym of the Homestead infuses the poem with despair. Even if anyone should ask for her hand 'of her Father', she would be beyond language, beyond even being able to signal 'acquiescence — or Demurral —'.

In the famous poem 'Because I could not stop for Death —/ He kindly stopped for me —', Dickinson's speaker is fetched away from where she lives. This solicitous suitor Death appears in 'Death is the supple Suitor' as one whose 'pallid innuendoes' will not be denied. Finally 'It bears away in triumph' its undescribed bride, in what Dickinson calls 'a bisected coach'. In 'Because I could not stop', Death is polite; he has all the time beyond the world. 'For His Civility', the speaker has 'put away/My labor and my leisure too'. In a stately coach they proceed outward from society, past nature, and beyond time.

> We passed the School, where Children strove
> At Recess — in the Ring —
> We passed the Fields of Gazing Grain —
> We passed the Setting Sun —
>
> Or, rather — He passed Us —

Although the coach is moving, it moves in a register that has stopped in relation to daily time. Here, the move from the house is a move out of time, and the uncanny house is the house of death, which resembles a fine mansion, but isn't.

Death as a lover is an old theme, traditionally applied by male poets to the death of young women; Schubert's 'Death and the Maiden' quartet is one Romantic version of the theme. The emotional reaction meant to be triggered by this set poetic topic was so widely accepted that Edgar Allen Poe in 'The Philosophy of Composition' chose it as the poetical topic *par excellence*. The difference from Dickinson's treatment could not be greater. Having decided that melancholy is the strongest emotion, Poe proceeds:

I asked myself — 'Of all melancholy topics, what, according to the *universal* understanding of mankind, is the *most* melancholy?' Death — was the obvious reply. 'And when,' I said, 'is this most melancholy of topics most poetical?' From what I have already explained at some length, the answer, here also, is obvious — 'When it most closely allies itself to *Beauty*: the death, then, of a beautiful woman is, unquestionably, the most poetical topic in the world — and equally it is beyond doubt that the lips best suited for such topic are those of a bereaved lover.'

Both Poe and Dickinson note a prurience connected with the death of women. In Poe it derives from the arousal which death provides for the onlooker and, through him, the reader; he orients such poems as 'The Raven' and 'Ulalume' towards the reader's pleasure in watching the spectacle of emotion and, perhaps, empathetically recreating it in tears.[5]

This stimulus-response pattern is, however, not universal, as Poe claims. A woman poet would be likely to see the eroticism of death from a different perspective. In the case of Sylvia Plath, a direct influence from Dickinson is likely. Dickinson's imagery of morbid courtship would seem to be the origin of the double image of death as father—lover and narcissist—lover in Plath's 'Death & Co'. Plath's first lover, sadistic and patriarchal behind his Blakean death-mask, tells the speaker 'how badly I photograph', how utterly she fails the representation-test of the male gaze. The second lover is narcissistically confident of his charms:

> His hair long and plausive
> Bastard
> Masturbating a glitter.

Plath projects her fear and rage onto the agent of seduction, while Dickinson is mute about the motives of death; only the repetition-pattern of his courtship is clear. In April 1953, Plath sent her mother some poems, remarking that 'any resemblance to Emily Dickinson is purely intentional'.[6]

For Dickinson the obscenity is found in death itself, which always assumes the success of its 'innuendo'. She doesn't relish the spectacle of death, because she experiences it from the inside. Later in 'Because I could not stop for Death —' the speaker realizes, as in a nightmare of sexual humiliation, that her clothing is transparent: 'Only Gossamer, my gown'. Her 'Tippet' [short cape] is 'only Tulle'. But, whatever the unveiling, she is once again being taken from one house to another:

> We paused before a House that seemed
> A Swelling of the Ground —
> The Roof was scarcely visible —
> The Cornice — in the Ground —

Dickinson doesn't depict her soul flying from her house to a home above. The ambiguous status of the house actually serves a surprising function as a hedge against dualism. If the question of where one is or how one locates oneself isn't easily answered, then that place is also not readily dismissed. Dickinson does not participate in nineteenth-century versions of seventeenth-century debates between body and soul such as Anne Bradstreet's 'The Flesh and the Spirit'. In Bradstreet's poem, the spirit denounces the flesh as its 'unregenerate part' and aspires to life in 'the City pure' of God. For Dickinson, the house never loses its freight of ambiguity. When Dickinson begins a poem with the lulling

> Sweet — safe — Houses —
> Glad — gay — Houses —
> Sealed so stately tight —

she is speaking of the tomb. When her female speaker writes of a home which is hers, it is a cottage-tomb. In one undated poem, 'The grave my little cottage is', she makes a 'marble tea' for her companion in death. In 'Wert thou but ill', declaring her readiness to serve her beloved in any way, she writes:

> The Tenant of the Narrow Cottage, wert Thou —
> Permit to be
> The Housewife in thy low attendance
> Contenteth Me —

In one late poem, 'To her derided Home', Dickinson has the

humble 'Weed of Summer' offer an answer, though a highly complex one, to the question of 'home'. Lack of consciousness protects the weed from suffering:

> To her derided Home
> A Weed of Summer came —
> She did not know her station low
> Nor Ignominy's Name —

Yet ignorance cannot be bliss, because it is without language. The second stanza shifts abruptly to the other side of the equation. Where is the language of joy to be found?

> Of Bliss the Codes are few —
> As Jesus cites of Him —
> 'Come unto me' the moiety
> That wafts the Seraphim —

Jesus offers joy, but to whom? Dickinson's answer is one of the most condensed in her poetry, perhaps because she is making herself consider the possibility of never having joy and knowledge together. The house of the weed is forgotten when the Father appears.

> All things are delivered unto me of my Father: and no man knoweth the Son, but the Father; neither knoweth any man the Father, save the Son, and he to whomsoever the Son will reveal him.
> Come unto me, all ye that labour and are heavy laden, and I will give you rest.
> (Matthew 11:27–8)

At the very moment when Jesus invites the sufferer to 'come unto him', he ascribes his authority to the Father. It is impossible for humankind ever to know Father or Son; only they know each other in an hermetic exchange. The weed cannot begin to enter into this relationship, and Dickinson cannot return to the blissful ignorance of the weed once she has found out about the hierarchy of the Father. Only at the point of death do the weed, the noble Lady and the seraphim share the potential of being wafted. This is a reason why Dickinson pauses so often to look at the transitional moment of death — only then are we between houses.

CHAPTER SEVEN

AN UNCANNY CONTAINER

Nature is a Haunted House — but Art — a House that tries to be haunted.
   (Letter to Thomas Wentworth Higginson, 1876, *Letters*, II, p. 554)

If we imagine Emily Dickinson making a tradition out of the circumference of her own practice, then her language tradition would be highly specific, word-orientated, metonymic, its syntax an active agent in generating meaning, its metaphors developing intertextually, in linked chains. The sensibility of the Dickinson tradition would arise from the drive towards knowledge, especially the personal knowledge of emotional honesty; it would think of itself as female; it would meditate on the immediate with the clear eye of Protestantism; it would try not to sublimate desire, even when desire hurts; and it would seek out those intermediate, borderline, and ambiguous states and places which go by the name of the uncanny. In theory at least, it might sometimes desire the transcendent, but in practice it would address itself to the way things are.

   This practice marks out a quite specific and original response to the problem of language, the transcendent, and the real. It separated Dickinson from her contemporaries. Whitman also worked out a mode of non-metaphysical language, but their solutions were different, and neither read the other. Metaphysics has come to mean the science — or philosophy — of that which is beyond the physical, even though its Greek root means a change or transfer, not an ascent. In the same way metaphor — literally, a change of what is being carried — has, in western practice, tended to mean something invisible (the signified) being represented by a simple or complex sense impression (the signifier). This view of metaphor, reinforced by idealist philosophy and Romantic poetry, was dominant in Emily Dickinson's day, and it formed the basis of Ralph Waldo Emerson's theory of poetic language.

Emerson remarked in his 1841 address, 'The Method of Nature', that there is 'something social and intrusive' in mere nature:

Therefore man must be on his guard against this cup of enchantments, and must look at nature with a supernatural eye. By piety alone, by conversing with the cause of nature, is he safe and commands it.[1]

In the Orphic vision, of which Orpheus the singer is one model and Zoroaster, the poet who founded a religion, is another, the beauty of nature in itself is too seductive, almost jostling to the poet. It is the 'Universal Power', which will not be seen face to face, to which the poet surrenders himself to become the agent of a higher knowledge. Dickinson never discusses inspiration as such. Nor does she prophesy or divine. She may be pure by intensity, but she consistently sees herself as low, dun, spotted – maculate rather than immaculate. She doesn't fit Emerson's definition of the poet, and her separateness requires proper space. When the Orphic mode is seen as the only line of American poetry, then Dickinson has no place at all, and what she has discovered is masked; she is a heretic to the Orphic creed, and that one thing is all that can ever be said of her.[2]

In 'The Poet', Emerson finds symbolism to be the route to transcendent knowledge. The symbol and thing symbolized can stand at a great distance from each other: 'Things admit of being used as symbols, because nature is a symbol, in the whole, and in every part' (*Essays and Lectures*, p. 452). At times Emerson allows for the material reality of nature; at other times he considers that only transcendent forms are true forms. In this mood he quotes with approval Edmund Spenser's declaration that the 'soul is form, and doth the body make'.

Emerson asserts the existence of a universal symbolic language in nature rather than in writing. In 'The Poet',

Beyond this universality of the symbolic language, we are apprised of the divineness of this superior use of things, whereby the world is a temple, whose walls are covered with emblems, pictures, and commandments of the Deity, in this, that there is no fact of nature which does not carry the whole sense of nature. . . .

(*Essays and Lectures*, p. 454)

The whole towards which all parts tend is the transcendent signified, God.

In the twentieth century much of the labour of American poetry has been addressed to the dismantling of Emerson's idealist heritage. For the male poet the struggle has been to develop a post-metaphysical poetics without losing the elevated role that Emerson gave to the Orphic poet-seer. Now that the theological basis for transcendent movement beyond the real has been eroded, there has been a struggle to find other modes of figuration which can express meaning by comparison, but without relying upon a transcendent signified. If Emily Dickinson's figurative language can be located, it may give shape to this more recent work. Very many of Dickinson's metaphors make startling connections or assertions; they resist interpretation, and many also do not have the intellectual play and self-consciousness of the conceit. She may write 'Bulb after Bulb, in Silver rolled' without having mentioned bulbs or silver in the poem. She may begin a poem with the cry 'Mine — by the Right of the White Election!' or 'Crisis is a Hair', and she may close it by introducing an entirely new series of connotations: 'Soundless as dots — on a Disc of Snow —'. She may attach words from one group of connotations to other quite different words without the slightest warning, as in 'the syllableless sea', 'staples in the Song', 'the heavens were stitched', 'a Sapphire farm', 'wearing the sod gown', wielding 'whip of diamond', or living 'Behind this soft Eclipse —'. There are hundreds of instances. Often these jolting switches from one field of connotation to another produce surreal sense-images as the two fields are superimposed in the reader's imagination.

In many of these demanding but very powerful combined images there doesn't seem to be any primacy of meaning given to the signified. Instead, the Dickinson ring or diadem of linked images may begin to establish itself, or there may be a kind of even exchange of figuration inside the particular poem. In the image of the 'whip of diamond', for example, both whip and diamond bring connotations to the vivid image, which expresses a particular sensation. The image isn't 'about' whips or diamonds. Dickinson's operating figure here may be the much maligned classical trope of metalepsis, or the metonymical substitution of one word for another, when both are figurative. Metalepsis is not a term in use today, even in specialized rhetorical criticism, because it has always been considered a fault. In Renaissance and neo-classical rhetoric one term of metaphor was expected to illustrate the other; the signifier served the signified. In metalepsis, however, the meaning travels back and forth between two words, or is packed into one word.

According to George Puttenham, the Elizabethan author of the rhetorical guide *The Arte of English Poesie* of 1589,

the sense is much altered and the hearers conceit strangely entangled by the figure *Metalepsis*, which I call the *farset*, as when we had rather fetch a word a great way off then to use one nerer hand to express the manner aswell and plainer.

Puttenham identifies metalepsis as a characteristically female trope, devised 'to please women'. He dislikes its habit of 'leaping over the heads of a great many words'. In an example he uses a female character:

Medea cursing her first acquaintance with prince *Iason*, who had very unkindly forsaken her, said:
  Woe worth the mountain that the maste bare
  Which was the first causer of all my care
Where she might aswell have said, woe worth our first meeting . . .[3]

Puttenham doesn't note that the 'leap' between mountain and

Jason is not mere bravado display or perversity, but arises from the vehemence of Medea's passion, which sees even the tree as laden with significant intent. Medea is expressing her emotional state with great accuracy by her use of a 'far set' metaphor which has gaps in reason built in. Metalepsis may be a 'feminine' trope because its distances accommodate the justified paranoia of the weak.

Dickinson's lifelong experiment in creating non-transcendent tropes was complicated by the fact that she continued at the same time to try out at least the possibility of transcendent meaning. The poem 'By my Window have I for Scenery' enacts a clash of the two systems, with God-sent 'Apprehensions' playing the concluding role; 'This World is not Conclusion' more typically reverses the process and shows doubt triumphing over the music of faith. Dickinson uses collections of analogies to approximate an issue;[4] her terminology is often highly specific, drawn from precise natural observation or from the terminology of botany, geology, astronomy or dressmaking. Yet her references — her signifieds — are usually either suppressed or left out; there is a denial of the historic dominance of the signified, and a consequent stress upon the poem as investigative or heuristic act. We may never find out what the pearls 'mean' in 'We play at Paste' but we soon come to understand the action of learning gem-tactics.

It is necessary to know all of Dickinson's work to know part of it fully. Her work as a whole provides the matrix in which the facets of the separate gems are revealed. Within a poem she circles around her question so that the circling creates the circumference which is itself a mode of knowledge. Perhaps the most accurate terminology for this setting of equals in a ring might be found, in keeping with Dickinson's own range, in zoology or chemistry. Her rings for groupings of similars might be called metamers, the technical chemical term for similar segments which, taken together, constitute larger bodies. Certainly her image of the diadem suggests something of atomic structure.

Like the image of the diadem, the trope of synechdoche implies that signifier and signified are part of the same entity;

not surprisingly, it has become a dominant device in modern American poetry. As Helen Vendler has pointed out,[5] Wallace Stevens's later poetry devolves around an expanded role for synechdoche in which the part signifying the whole becomes a way by which terms such as 'planet' or 'sun', hitherto associated with metaphysical signification, can be rescued into a discourse of the real.

Not that this expanded synechdoche was entirely alien to Emerson; in the passage from 'The Poet' quoted above, Emerson is saying that every fact of nature carries the whole meaning of nature. Each leaf, in other words, is synechdochic for Nature (nature-as-meaning). The difference lies in the fact that Emerson attributed authority for that meaning to the Deity beyond nature. In Stevens the effort is to make the sun a whole of which, say, the first birdsong of spring could be a part.

Dickinson's emotional honesty meant that she regularly brought her art to bear upon intense and complex emotions, attempting this mode of address even when, as in the case of the house, what she is addressing is not so much before her as around, behind her, and part of her even as she is part of it. Much modern American poetry has concentrated upon the image as the clearest route forward out of all-enveloping symbolism. Yet many areas of our experience have the ambiguous status of the Dickinson house. Consider all those aspects of experience which are 'others', but not quite representable, which press in from the edge upon the visible, which are part thought about, part repressed. In a transcendent model, that which is outside the visible must be either above or below it. But in Dickinson's poems of fixed perspective, there is much that is outside of frame, to the sides, hidden, behind, inside. These borderline areas are defined by the mysteries which limit and define life while being part of all life, namely the mysteries of birth and death. These are the ghosts which live in our own house. The sensation we have glimpsing the trace of these borderline events has a name, and that name stands, appropriately, between literature and psychoanalysis. It is the uncanny.

An exploration of this term, the uncanny, may give us a terminology (or a terminological structure) which may enable us to see just where Dickinson's heuristic quest is going. The uncanny of birth is gender-specific, and Dickinson's use of it is important for the womanly mode of learning about where one lives.

Sigmund Freud's article 'The "Uncanny" ' (1919) is a literary-theoretical essay: what he describes is a literary sensation. A major part of his essay is devoted to a précis and analysis of E. T. A. Hoffmann's tale 'The Sand-Man', and almost all of the instances cited are literary, rather than case histories. Considering the detective–scientist persona that Freud gives himself in his case histories, 'The "Uncanny" ' is also a curiously uncertain piece of writing, rather rambling, exhibiting the same kind of relation to its topic that experience itself bears to the uncanny.

According to Freud, 'The uncanny is that class of the frightening which leads us back to what is known of old and long familiar.' Significantly, he begins with an action of going inside the word, investigating its etymology and usage, rather than proceeding directly to using the word as a symbol. In German the sensation of the uncanny is known as *das Unheimliche*, but certain meanings of its apparent antonym, *heimlich*, also carry connotations of the sinister, the secret, the hidden inside or connected with what is known. The opposites of 'unhomelike' and 'homelike' attract. In this way the ambivalence of the uncanny is expressed by its appearance in words of quite opposite meaning.

Freud locates uncanny sensations in the experience of borderline phenomena such as the automaton, on the borderline between the human and the mechanical; or the double, between the subject (oneself) and the other. It also occurs in the compulsion to repeat, especially a circular movement; in the 'evil eye'; in the belief in the omnipotence of thoughts; in the dead, especially inside houses; and in the fear of being buried alive. Freud's list looks provisional. I would also add that the sensation of the uncanny is associated with the failure or disappearance of clock time, and with very sharp sight, with looking as closely as one can at the phenomenon. It seems to be a product of modern civilization, despite its connections with animistic belief. Uncanny events do not occur in classical myth or in primitive folk-tale because the relation of natural to supernatural is known; it is in the interstices of doubt that the uncanny enters.

Although Freud devotes most of his literary analysis to Hoffman's use of automatons and doubles, his initial discussion has firmly located the root of uncanniness in the home (*das Heim*). For Freud, such a startling and unwished-for experience as the uncanny must represent an eruption of the repressed into daily life. He seizes upon Schelling's dictionary definition that *Unheimlich* is the name for 'everything that ought to have remained . . . secret and hidden but has come to light.' The quintessential uncanny experience for man has been life in his first home, the womb, where he was both himself but not himself, both a whole and a part, inside his mother's body without being there sexually:

To some people the idea of being buried alive by mistake is the most uncanny thing of all. And yet psychoanalysis has taught us that this terrifying fantasy is only a transformation of another fantasy which had originally nothing terrifying about it at all, but was qualified by a certain lasciviousness — the fantasy, I mean, of intra-uterine existence.[6]

This recognition goes back much further than Freud. Job cries in his extremity, 'Naked came I out of my mother's womb, and naked shall I return thither' (Job 1:21). The womb (symbolically, Mother Earth) receives us once again in its second role as tomb. Job, however, speaks without calling attention to any symbol.

Freud presses his case home, using, as one might expect, male examples to define the sexual uncanny:

It often happens that neurotic men declare that they feel there is something uncanny about the female genital organs. This *unheimlich* place, however, is the entrance to the former *Heim* [home] of all human beings, to the place where each one of us lived once upon a time and in the beginning. . . . the *unheimlich* is what was once *heimisch*, familiar; the prefix '*un*' is the token of repression. (Vol. 14, p. 368)

If our first home was our mother's body, we are all exiles, but men are more exiles than women. Since women embody the mystery of containment out of which they sprung, it is never wholly outside them; they inhabit it. Their uncanny can be familiar. The house, with its womb-like containment, can be frighteningly uncanny for men; historically this fear has been allayed by men owning the house. In Poe's tale 'The Fall of the House of Usher' the house is both a metonym for the Usher family and the literal house. In Poe, the house falls because it has a woman buried in its bowels.

For the woman writer the house must carry the conflicting configuration that Dickinson works out so painstakingly: one's own and not one's own, male and female, past and present.

Elizabeth Bishop's early poem 'The Monument' creates an uncanny structure whose signification floats between art work, pile of junk, and monument. It is 'like' them all, without ever quite being anything. 'The Monument' is a poem of fixed perspective — looked at, it won't reveal its inside: 'it may be solid, may be hollow'. It may be the tomb of an artist—prince, it may be a temple. Having drawn her circle of signification, Bishop concludes 'Watch it closely', for it is from ambiguous structures such as this that art comes. In 'House for the Rainy Season', a poem of praise for her own house in Brazil, Bishop acquaints us with a female uncanny house, 'familiar unbidden', hidden, laden with plant and animal life, especially animals escaped from the gothic: owl, frog, silverfish, mouse, moth and — her joke — bookworms. In terms which recall those Dickinson uses for her body, but with a warmth that the Dickinson house never has, Bishop makes her woman-house 'darkened and tarnished . . . maculate, cherished'.

In the gothic, some of the ghosts have been left there by a withdrawing God; others have always lived there. Dickinson's poems have very few ghosts for their period, but when a ghost appears, it is linked with the uncanny theme of the double. In a self-consciously literary poem Dickinson writes:

One need not be a Chamber — to be Haunted —
One need not be a House —
The Brain has Corridors — surpassing
Material Place —

In this internalized gothic, 'Far safer, through an Abbey gallop'. At home, the fear is of becoming doubled: 'Oneself behind ourself, concealed —/Should startle most —'.

Some of Dickinson's most moving poems accept that ghosts, or memories, live in the house with her in a kind of natural uncanniness. Certainly such part-creatures appear more frequently than her family in Dickinson's house poems. In 'Of nearness to her sundered Things', Dickinson depicts the moments when past and present flow together, and both can be contained within the house:

Of nearness to her sundered Things
The Soul has special times —
When Dimness — looks the Oddity —
Distinctness — easy — seems —

The dead return in moments of clarity, not darkness. The 'Mouldering Playmate' reappears just as he was when 'we — old mornings, Children — played —' (this is a less morbid image than it may seen, since many of the close friends of Emily's girlhood and youth did die young). With the interior space of the house illuminated and altered by a commanded, known, surreally flexible time, death too must reverse itself and give back Emily's friends:

The Grave yields back her Robberies —
The Years, our pilfered Things —
Bright Knots of Apparitions
Salute us, with their wings —

Dickinson's house poems do not have to evoke the gothic or ghosts to use the uncanny, since it is pre-eminently the mode of looking at container and contained. For Dickinson, as a woman poet, the container is not represented as something waiting to be filled. Dickinson's repeated forays on the meta-phoric territory of the house are about knowledge that is inside or on the borderline. This is the equivalent in imag-ery to the rhetorical tropes of metonymy, synechdoche, even metalepsis. Since language is one of the workings-out of a psychic economy, this similar structuring should be expected, though perhaps the intensity with which Dickinson investigates it has been necessary before it can be recognized.

Dickinson prompts a speculation. Perhaps there are two basic models of thinking figuratively in language. One in-volves representation, depiction, symbolization, the known and the unknown, this as that. Then there is another, involving sameness, container and contained, circumference. The tradi-tional imagery of symbolism is the imagery of our culture. The imagery of the uncanny container uses many of the same objects, but differently: the house, the body, especially the woman's body with its womb (Pandora's Box), the temple, the monument, the tomb, the coffin, the closet, the reliquary, the pack or parcel, the bowl, the nest, the sunken ship, the beehive, the book, the cave, the mine, the sea and, within the sea, the submarine.

In the opening stanza of her poem 'Daddy', Sylvia Plath depicts the body of her father as an 'old shoe', which is also a house. And the aquarium, the car, the ditch, the safe and the television set are all explored by Robert Lowell in his container-poem 'For the Union Dead'. Lowell's poem is a deliberately secular look at contemporary Boston, and there is a deep, purposeful hostility between the uncanny and reli-gious mystery in the Christian tradition. The wine in the container of the communion chalice is not that wine, it is something entirely different, the blood of Christ. The wafer is not the wafer. The tropes of containment imply that what we see may be connected with other things, but it is always itself. It often has things hidden, but they are inside. From the uncanny container we are not far from the ritual objects of paganism, of which the reliquary comes closest: the voodoo object, the embalmed body, the frozen body or plant, taxidermy. In these something is magical or terrifying because it is made up of a real thing which hasn't been transformed, though it has had to be killed for its magic to be used. Perhaps Dickinson, in her magic prison, sometimes used her own life this untransformed way.[7]

CHAPTER EIGHT

THE SISTER

Sister,
   We both are Women, and there is a Will of God — Could the
Dying confide Death, there would be no Dead — Wedlock is
shyer than Death. Thank you for Tenderness —
   I find it is the only food that the Will takes, nor that from
general fingers — I am glad you go — It does not remove you —
I seek you first in Amherst, then turn my thoughts without a
Whip — so well they follow you —
   (Emily Dickinson to Susan Gilbert Dickinson, *Letters*, II,
   p. 445)

Emily Dickinson may have felt that she had 'no mother', but
she did have sisters, and she treasured them. Her sense of
herself as a woman amongst women was so central to both her
personal and literary existence that it is difficult to imagine how
she could have survived without it. Before discussing Dickinson's female relationships, I have wanted to show just how all-
encompassing her sense of herself as woman writer actually
was; I have wanted her poetry to prove her 'difference' on its
own. This chapter continues to look at the Dickinson model of
knowledge, but from the point of view of the woman writer in
the nineteenth century. It is a view from the inside, from what
I take to have been Dickinson's deep acceptance of her sex.
   Dickinson not only wrote consciously as a woman, she saw
herself as part of a female poetic sisterhood. There are many
traditions active in Dickinson's work, but this was the one she
identified with most strongly. Many qualities of her work are
shared with other women writers, even though our education

in the gender-based canon has meant that this female tradition has remained virtually invisible.

As we recover Dickinson, we recover the sisterly. As a consequence, looking back at Dickinson and her sisters also points forward and changes the perspective from which we may read other writers. For the woman wanting to write now, or wanting to understand the experience of her sex through reading, knowledge of a female tradition is a psychological necessity. Otherwise we each write alone. Since Dickinson encountered her femaleness directly, both as woman and as writer, her life and work are a natural focus for any creative understanding of sex, the social gendering of sex, and poetic knowledge. Her fierce power sets a standard for which no one need apologize. It is entirely appropriate that Dickinson's relations to her female contemporaries and forebears constitute one of the most fruitful areas of feminist scholarship today.

The first, essential recognition about Dickinson's sisterly relations is that she did not live alone, either personally or culturally. She lived with her sister Vinnie, she fell in love with women just as deeply as with men, and throughout her life she maintained a lively exchange of letters, poems and gifts with women neighbours, relatives and friends. When Dickinson wrote about the poet as type, she tended to cast herself in the role of passive, appreciative reader. 'Poet' as type is masculinized; 'reader' behaves femininely. The poet as type is a noble, illuminating man who lived in the past. To lead into Dickinson's views about women writers, we should first consider her views about male poets.

Shakespeare always formed the core of Dickinson's reading, serving as the touchstone for poetic range. Dickinson also enjoyed reading many of the standard male authors of her day. We never find her attacking male writers as a group.[1] She did not, however, suffer gladly the inflated, generalized poetic diction of the conservative poetic establishment:

A few incisive Mornings —
A few ascetic Eves —
Gone — Mr. Bryant's 'Golden Rod'
And Mr. Thomson's 'sheaves'.

Dickinson's sarcasm is particularly pointed here, since she is attacking the English pre-Romantic Thomson, who wrote the long meditative—descriptive poem 'The Seasons', and William Cullen Bryant, an American follower of Wordsworth, whose poem 'The Death of the Flowers' describes the golden rod. Both Thomson and Bryant were famous nature poets whose fame, Dickinson indicates, was not based on any great ability to observe nature.[2]

Dickinson disliked the metaphysical assumptions which were meant to lend authority to Romantic philosophical poetry. In an 1866 letter to Mrs J. G. Holland, a close friend whom she often addressed as 'sister', Dickinson refers with some condescension to Wordsworth's famous 'Elegaic Stanzas':

> February passed like a Skate and I know March. Here is the 'light' the Stranger said was 'was not on land or sea'. Myself could arrest it but we'll not chagrin Him. . . .
>
> The Wind blows gay today and the Jays bark like Blue Terriers. I tell you what I see. The Landscape of the Spirit requires a lung, but no Tongue.
>
> (*Letters*, II, pp. 449–50)

The implication is that Wordsworth, 'the Stranger', wrote about what he couldn't see; Dickinson could easily outpace him because she writes with lucid metaphor about what she does see. Dickinson seems also to be questioning Wordsworth's assertion that the appropriate role of the poet is to add the veneer of the invisible 'gleam' to the accepted, framed perspective of the painter.[3]

When Dickinson turns to nineteenth-century women and women writers, her attitude changes completely. On the personal level, she wrote to Sue, sincerely but with appropriate ambiguity, 'With the exception of Shakespeare, you have told me of more knowledge than any one living' (*Letters*, III, p. 733). The beloved sister 'a hedge away', as she put it in 'One Sister have I in our house', gives Dickinson a knowledge which is just as profound — and by implication, just as shot through with admixtures of good and evil — as the knowledge given by all of Shakespeare.

Replying in 1871 to Higginson's questions about recent poetry, Dickinson dismissed the forced sublimity of Joaquin Miller's *Songs of the Sierras* and then homed in on women's poetry as genre:

I did not read Mr Miller because I could not care about him —
Transport is not urged —
Mrs Hunt's Poems are stronger than any written by Women since Mrs
— Browning, with the exception of Mrs Lewes — but Truth like
Ancestor's Brocades can stand alone —

(*Letters*, II, p. 491)

Women's poetry, she indicates, has its own standards, its own context. Although Dickinson prefers Elizabeth Barrett Browning, she tries not to denigrate George Eliot, referring politely to her by the name she would have had if she and Lewes had been married. Then she weaves in a homage to George Eliot by paraphrasing a passage from *Adam Bede* to indicate that truth (like a good poet) does not need to be compared to other truth. It stands alone.

When Dickinson describes women writers she knows only through their writing, she is as immediate in her concern as if they were intimates. She is not only well-informed and enthusiastic about recent women's writing, she expresses great empathy with the conditions of the writers' lives. When a woman writer she admires dies, Dickinson writes about the death in terms which she otherwise reserves for close friends and family members. In this almost presumptuous curiosity, she shows most clearly her identification with women writers as a group. For her they are 'family'.

Dickinson appears to have enjoyed female 'sensation' writing, such as the stories of Harriet Prescott Spofford, quite as much as more critically accepted women's writing. With women poets or poems which we might assume she could not praise, she is supportively silent. Both Dickinson's letters and her poems were supporting that nineteenth-century creative literary feminism which Ellen Moers has called 'heroinism'.[4] Women who had survived family and social pressure, and who wrote explicitly as women, had nothing but praise from Dickinson, even when her views and poetic practice differed from theirs. What Dickinson was concerned with was what we would call today the relation between gender and literary production – an issue which her own work raises.

One apparent difference between Dickinson and her literary sisters yields a similarity. Sandra Gilbert and Susan Gubar have written about an anxiety of gender which women felt when they sought to enter the male-controlled realm of literary language. Being women, how could they be worthy? Many women writers gained access to literary language by devoting their talent to some ideal or duty beyond the personal: Christianity, abolition of slavery, nationalism, child labour, education, temperance, Indian rights, women's rights, or the very idea of vocation itself (as in George Eliot). That way they could escape from the fear that their writing was merely the cry of their female condition – or that it would *seem* to be merely such a cry. By not publishing, Dickinson avoided this anxiety. But Dickinson, a well-educated American, always had an easier relationship with writing than her English sisters, especially in the light of Emerson's attacks upon received tradition. Dickinson confirms her claim to language by separating out the written and inhabiting it. Yet she too writes out of a devotion to something beyond herself, when she writes in a quite undisplaced way about her feelings and about what she sees. Whether or not this will look weakly feminine doesn't concern her. Her 'work' is to find out all she can, using her unsublimated female self as agency for this knowledge.

The mid-century literary scene seems to have looked to Emily Dickinson like a dawning of women's expression. She doesn't refer to a female literary past, except for Sappho. While she might have read Anne Bradstreet, her American Puritan precursor, she doesn't cite her or other earlier women writers in English, such as Anne Finch, Countess of Winchelsea, Fanny Burney or Mary Wollstonecraft. For both practical and theoretical purposes her literary past is male. She does not, however, seem to perceive the lack of a past as a problem, since she sees the present she is writing in as pre-eminently female. This was both a polemic and an accurate view.

Dickinson's main 'heroines' were Elizabeth Barrett Browning, the Brontë sisters, George Eliot and George Sand — titanic literary figures whose triumph against adversity was a model for the younger woman writer. All these women were immensely respected, even when their lives or ideas were heterodox. As Dickinson wrote of George Eliot after Eliot's death:

> Her losses make our Gains ashamed —
> She bore Life's empty Pack
> As gallantly as if the East
> Were swinging at her Back.

This was Dickinson's kind of heroism. It had nothing to do with heroic self-image or heroic quest.

The mid nineteenth-century construct of women's writing has some telling parallels with the psychological construction of the House of Dickinson. The father controls the past, money and the law, which he represents. For the young woman, love for the Master means silence and disappearance into the role of audience, even though (as Ellen Moers notes) a paternal figure may be a temporary help. There is no mother. That loss is never filled. If there is a brother, he leaves when childhood ends.[5] Instead, there are many inspiring, vivid sisters, some older, some contemporary, whose life is like one's own. Like oneself, these sisterly figures do not separate life and art; cannot and will not separate it. Born at the wrong time, Dickinson was also born at the right time. The female literary scene was a ready-made, oddly *economical* answer to the Oedipal dilemma that Dickinson faced. Love for the literary sister was a breakaway from the Oedipal family romance; the older sister may guide, but she guides as a more experienced equal. Learning from her leads into present and future; indeed, the act of learning from another woman can represent the necessary self-acceptance and maturity which the younger woman needs to aim her will to write. As Dickinson wrote to Sue, sisterly tenderness 'is the only food that the Will takes, nor that from general fingers'.

And, for Dickinson at least, there is only a sister. Emily Dickinson had a brother, a sensitive and intelligent man whom she dearly loved. But Austin does not enter the poems. The intimate sibling pair is not part of her poetic construct. The absence of the mother also projects forward an absence of children. The poet herself may not be able to be a mother to the next generation. While this might be expected in a childless poet like Dickinson, it holds for Elizabeth Barratt Browning and others as well. Dickinson's sense of her female body informs her imagery of uncanny containers, and includes the bosom, the freckled or 'dun' skin, the 'low' body, the portal, gap and 'valves' of vaginal imagery, and the bare feet as synechdoche for both humility and nakedness. But the body is not seen as bearing children. Elizabeth Barratt Browning, who did have a child, seems to have come to the same conclusion by opposite means. In 'A Woman and A Poet', *Aurora Leigh* and other poems, she sees female fecundity and suckling as being used by men to deny spiritual fecundity in women — and she sees this attitude surviving her.

Elizabeth Barrett Browning (1806—61) was Emily Dickinson's central heroine, the woman poet whose youth most closely resembled her own. Though the young Elizabeth Barrett was English, urban and found the space to write by being a pampered invalid, both Dickinson and she were eldest daughters and the favourite of wealthy fathers who wanted their children to stay at home forever. Elizabeth Barrett's mother died young; Dickinson's was ineffectual. Both poets were well-educated. Barrett's tutorial education, while narrower, proceeded further than Dickinson's, into classical scholarship and translation. In the mid 1840s the patterns of the poets' lives diverged poignantly, as Barrett's considerable fame brought her an admirer, Robert Browning, who eloped with her in her fortieth year.

The moment of first looking into Elizabeth Barrett Browning is, for Dickinson, the first moment of vocation:

> I think I was enchanted
> When first a sombre Girl —
> I read that Foreign Lady —
> The Dark — felt beautiful —

The effect of reading her is metamorphic rather than trans-cendent: 'The Bees — became as Butterflies — . . . The Days — to Mighty Metres stept —'. In terms which echo the 'gold thread' letter, Dickinson declares that once she has experienced this 'Lunacy of Light' she will forever prefer 'Divine Insanity' to what she terms 'the Danger to be Sane'.

Elizabeth Barrett Browning believed fervently in many causes: the unification of Italy (in the collection *Casa Guidi Windows*) and an end to child labour (in 'The Cry of the Children') were only two. Dickinson went directly to the magic which underlies the immediate passion of her poetry — whatever Elizabeth Barrett Browning wrote about, the effect is of a sparkling, passionate energy transforming everything into poetry. According to Dickinson, this power is not so much literary as magical: the woman writer as witch.[6] If she is threatened by sanity, Dickinson concludes, the acolyte will turn

> To Tomes of solid Witchcraft —
> Magicians be asleep —
> But Magic — hath an Element
> Like Deity — to keep —

These Tomes are the female poetic texts.

The great cause uniting all others for Barrett Browning was, in fact, 'heroinism' itself. She shared one of her own inspiring heroines with Dickinson, beginning the fiery sonnet 'To George Sand: A Desire' with the accolade: 'Thou large-brained woman and large-hearted man/Self-called George Sand!' Like Dickinson in 'I'm ceded — I've stopped being Theirs', Barrett Browning praises the woman who takes her own name. In the next sonnet, 'To George Sand: A Recognition', she stresses that the re-named writer is still a woman. 'That revolted cry/Is sobbed in by a woman's voice forlorn —':

> while before
> The world, thou burnest in a poet-fire,
> We see thy woman-heart burn evermore,
> Through the large flame.

Whether or not the robust Sand was 'forlorn', Barrett Browning sexes and socially genders her at once: to be a woman is to sob and suffer. This element of pain, she indicates, is innate. Dickinson also slightly Victorianizes Sand, perceptively liking this type with Barrett Browning herself:

That Mrs. Browning fainted, we need not read *Aurora Leigh* to know, when she lived with her English aunt; and George Sand 'must make no noise in her grandmother's bedroom.' Poor children! Women, now, queens, now! And one in the Eden of God.
   (*Letters*, II, p. 376)

In both poem and letter Dickinson is paying another allusive homage to Barrett Browning, whose heroine Aurora Leigh is described as having been ignored 'Because she was a woman and a queen,/And had no beard to bristle through her song' (Book VIII, 331–2).

   In her verse novel *Aurora Leigh*, which Dickinson seems virtually to have known by heart, Barrett Browning traces the maturation of her poet heroine, named Aurora after Aurora Dupin, Sand's real name. After listing male assumptions about woman's proper role and showing Aurora refusing a marriage to her cousin Romney, Barrett Browning has her heroine turn female qualities into necessities for great poetry. This is Aurora's credo:

>   Never flinch,
> But still, unscrupulously epic, catch
> Upon the burning lava of a song
> The full-veined, heaving, double-breasted Age:
> That, when the next shall come, the men of that
> May touch the impress with reverent hand, and say
> 'Behold, – behold the paps we all have sucked
> This bosom seems to beat still, or at least
> It sets our beating: this is living art,
> Which thus presents and thus records true life.'
>   (Book V, 214–22)

As Ellen Moers has commented, those double breasts of the Age are women's breasts; even more outrageously, literary influence is represented as men feeling the 'lava' of a breast at which they have suckled. The poet is female, her future audience is, interestingly, male. There is still no female tradition. Dickinson's volcano imagery has a powerful antecedent in this passage: the heaving breast is transformed into the lava of song. 'This is living art', indeed, with a flood of metaphors welling out from their source in the body of woman.

To the modern reader, this passage may seem excessively opulent, its metaphors insufficiently separated from each other. The same problem afflicts modern readers of the lush body/food imagery of Christina Rossetti's 'Goblin Market'. In *Aurora Leigh*, the flowing lava seems a transference of breast milk while also being the breast; what is being touched is both the naturally formed mould (female art) and the breast of the woman herself. In fact, these joinings are deliberate; what is daunting about the passage is its joining of an uncompromising female poetics with lush erotic imagery. Lava is a precise image for something which takes sculptural shape naturally, like female art as Barrett Browning saw it.

Barrett Browning asserts that her lush poem is her feelings. Her poetry recapitulates emotion by the imitative form of heightened, exclamatory diction. As she wrote in her sonnet, 'The Soul's Expression', her struggle is to 'deliver right/That music of my nature'. Dickinson praises agony because it communicates authentically. She writes much more ascetically than Browning; her poetics of circumference differs strongly from Browning's transcendent symbolism, and her range of lyric form is decidedly smaller but, like Barrett Browning, she doesn't distance the anguish of the poem from the anguish of the woman:

> I felt my life with both my hands
> To see if it was there —

Or, with devastating precision:

> I felt a Funeral, in my Brain,
> And Mourners to and fro
> Kept treading — treading — till it seemed
> That Sense was breaking through —

The question arises as to the status of this directly expressed feeling. Do these women poets represent a kind of apogee of emotionalism, of romantic failure to distinguish between emotion and literature? In his essay 'Tradition and the Individual Talent', T. S. Eliot laid down a line for 'impersonal' modernism which would severely condemn such minglings. The poet, Eliot argued, must distinguish between literary emotion and mere personal feelings, which are of no interest to anyone but the poet himself. Eliot was attacking romanticism in general, but his attack would fall hardest upon the unmediated presence of the woman's feeling in poems by Dickinson, Barrett Browning, Rossetti, or dozens of lesser woman poets of the nineteenth century. The emotional directness which women writers themselves used to define women's poetry was a quality which modernism felt it most essential to avoid.

Women poets may have suffered from the consequences of an all too successful pursuit of aspects of Romanticism. Romanticism had involved a Promethean or Byronic hero, a grasping of the poetic mantle — all the panoply and anguish of the bardic singer. Emerson's Orphic poet aims for centrality, but the model is the same. In his quest for full existence, Romantic man embraced a life of feeling. Women poets did so as well, noting that access to feeling was already considered a feminine attribute.

Yet in men's image of women, the active half of the Romantic personality was missing. As Nina Baym has pointed out in *Women's Fiction*, women's literary perception of women's lives concerned work, money, self-respect and the need for endurance and strength in adversity. This view of female heroism was not reinforced by the male literary image of woman, particularly in poetry. 'Heroinism' itself — that strength to survive and write as a woman — was a phenomenon that had to be re-created with each female literary generation.

As repeated waves of political reaction brought home to European poets the futility of political engagement, modes of feeling offered a retreat. Heine's irony and Baudelaire's spleen offered bracing negatives, but the clearest route was that already taken by many women poets, into feeling as limit, feeling as acceptance, feeling as evasion. Many readers of nineteenth-century poetry have noted that the field of poetry shrank disastrously as the century wore on; but it decreased, as it were, in the direction of the feminine. Typically, absence or lack in the present was displaced into the past — lost love, lost childhood, lost beauty — and it was expressed as melancholy, as in Poe's theory and practice. In the United States, Emerson brilliantly halted this drift towards what was perceived as the feminine by claiming his aesthetic of the eye for the masculine. The more Emerson is writing about poet or scholar expressing the beautiful or about how he must pause to let the influx of nature and natural symbolism pervade him — the more, in other words, his poet—hero exhibits 'feminine' qualities — the more insistently and imperially male Emerson genders that hero. Emerson does not posit a poetic androgyny, even one in which the masculine is the dominant element. It was against this formulation that Dickinson had to make headway.

We are most familiar with psychological gendering through Freud's pernicious correlation of socially gendered passive and emotional femininity with the female sex *per se*. At the same time Freud gendered intellect and will male. Yet Freud's assumption was only a late instance of a gendering familiar to any reader of literature in the nineteenth century. In the preface to *Female Poets of America* (1849, revised edition 1873) the first collection of women's poetry in the United States, Rufus Griswold excused his exercise on the grounds that intellectual, abstract male genius needed to be tempered by the access to feeling which he considered characteristic of the feminine sensibility. In other words, he had chosen his women poets for the way they exemplified his pre-existing views of what was feminine. In his headnotes to the actual poems, Griswold often had only the faintest of praise for the poems he selected, finding them weak, narrowly emotional and form-ally undeveloped — in other words, feminine.

In the 1890s the influential American critic and poet Edmund Clarence Stedman praised female lyric for its quint-essential femininity:

The artistic temperament is, after all, androgynous. The woman's intuition, sensitiveness, nervous refinement join with the reserved power and creative vigor of the man to form the poet. . . . The revelations of the feminine heart are the more beautiful and welcome, because the typical woman is purer, more unselfish, more consecrated, than the typical man.

According to Stedman, male confessional poetry is less attractive, but the more 'like a child' a woman writes, directly and with feeling, the more 'our ideals of sanctity are maintained'. Stedman does not mean to condescend:

Mrs Browning's lyrics, every verse sealed with her individuality, glowing with sympathy, and so unselfconsciously and unselfishly displaying the nobility of her heart and intellect, have made the earth she trod sacred. . . . The 'Sonnets from the Portuguese' at the extreme of proud self-avowal, are equal in beauty, feeling, and psychical analysis to any series of sonnets in any tongue, — Shakespeare not excepted.[8]

I have quoted Stedman at some length because, except for a mistake about unselfconsciousness, his description of Barrett Browning cuts very close to the bone. The triumph of her poetry was in fact to make claims for the female without diverging from what was expected of the socially feminine (presumably Stedman, like most readers, found her social poems less interesting). Other women poets were less dextrous than Barrett Browning in balancing the identity which had been chosen with the identity which had been imposed.

Since Dickinson's public silence liberated her from the feminine double bind of distorting one's identity every time one seeks to express it, her work exemplified one way of writing as a woman without compromise. Dickinson shared Barrett Browning's commitment to direct feeling; her patriarchal analysis was, if anything, more bitterly incisive than Barrett Browning's. In many areas, such as her elliptical syntax and her choice of imagery, Dickinson's practice seems to ignore possible accusations of the merely feminine while also keeping a great distance from the more emotional tone of her female contemporaries, including Barrett Browning.

The idea of women's poetry as women's work gave Dickinson an opportunity to examine conflicts of inner and imposed senses of the womanly. Dickinson's preferred metaphor for her poetics of linked facets was the hard, shining gem mined from the earth, or the queenly diadem. When she uses imagery of stitching (joining fabric together) and weaving (making cloth), she refers to the weaving together of the literary text, as in the 'gold thread' letter. At the same time, sewing imagery also refers to the low valuation of female loom work, and to the mockery of creative work in feminine-gendered, socially approved needlework. Sewing and its related terms are Janus-words in Dickinson, but not because of conflicting connotative potential in the words themselves. Rather it is society which reads a social function into sewing. This closeness of set function may have been what limited her use of the sewing metaphor. As a consequence of this social discourse, however, her poems about sewing are a particularly rich source for her distinctions between female and feminine, between the inner-determined diadem of meaning and the socially agreed meaning.

In one poem, 'Don't put up my Thread and Needle –', the speaker's struggle to sew 'Better Stitches – so' is movingly connected with Dickinson's well-founded fear of going blind. One must see in order to sew, whether it is textile or text. Yet even if she recovers to sew at all, her poetic 'work' will converge insidiously with the gender-linked fancy-work (on textiles and texts alike) with which Victorian middle-class women passed the time. The poem develops its metaphors along a connotative knife-edge of valuable and idle work. The speaker apologises that her stitches have been 'bent' because 'my sight got crooked', but the regret may be for insufficient perception or, in conventional terms, insufficiently regular metric.

'When my mind – is plain', the speaker continues, internalizing sight to insight, she'll 'do seams – a Queen's endeavor/ Would not blush to own –'. This metaphor is a facet of

Dickinson's diadem-imagery, in which, through high art and passion, she becomes a self-crowned Queen. It also can be read in terms of prevailing social discourse, as that inversion of 'endeavour' which was time-consuming embroidery. Particularly in the Victorian era, 'work' meant 'the operation of making a textile fabric or (more usually) something consisting of such fabric', and the term was mildly derogatory when feminized: '*esp.*, any of the lighter of the operations of this kind, as a distinctively feminine operation'.[9]

Alert to the inexorable double meaning of 'work' in social discourse, Dickinson describes her own literary work ambivalently: she can create

> Hems — too fine for Lady's tracing
> To the sightless Knot —
> Tucks — of dainty interspersion —
> Like a dotted Dot —

The 'sightless Knot' is a brilliant instance of the kind of linguistic condensation which it represents: Dickinson's poems knot meanings together so skilfully that the technique is invisible. The tucks — compressions and ellipses — are signatures of a Dickinson 'work'. But here the other face of 'work' intrudes its connotations: the interspersions are 'dainty' and, more sinisterly, the 'work' may be so tiny (the poems so short and finely wrought) that they may be trivial, 'like a dotted Dot —'. Even if angels are dancing on the head of a pin, it is still just a pin.

'Just' is, in fact, one of Dickinson's most frequently used words, appearing 244 times in her poetry. 'Just' in the sense of 'merely' or 'only' is an essential Dickinson word because it modestly makes its very small claims to significance while simultaneously operating in invisible inverted commas to indicate the opposite of modesty. Many of Dickinson's poems display staggering leaps of proportion from tiny to sublime as displays of epistemological range.

In 'Dont put up my Thread and Needle —' the speaker's physical exhaustion leaves the poem's proportion-play in miniature. Her 'work' may indeed be no more than women's

work is said to be. Leaving the poem in miniature but continuing its vocative plea, apparently to a woman, the speaker asks
that her needle be left, as a plough is left, 'in the furrow' for
her return:

> I can make the zigzag stitches
> Straight — when I am strong —
>
> Till then — dreaming I am sewing
> Fetch the seam I missed —
> Closer — so I — at my sleeping —
> Still surmise I stitch —

In calling her sewing-dream 'surmise', Dickinson is titling it
with a term for sublime but highly conscious thought; perhaps
she is also echoing the 'wild surmise' in Keat's 'On First
Looking into Chapman's Homer' of discoverers who don't yet
have a name for what they see.

'Don't put up my Thread and Needle —' located the Dickinson speaker firmly in the world of woman's work. She neither
wishes to transcend or ignore her sex; her 'work' is different
but the way all women's labour is degraded trivializes her own
work too. When creative work runs the risk of being read
according to society's image of the author's sex (or race or
class), the writer's formal strategies are put under immense
pressure. In the case of the nineteenth-century poets, she could
adhere to the feminine. She could outwardly keep to feminine
convention while subverting it and using it as an instrument of
self-expression or rebellion. She could invade hitherto male
forms such as epic, dramatic poetry or the sonnet, and take
them over for her female discourse. Or she could invent new
forms, sexed or (at least in aspiration) unsexed. All of these
strategies were used by nineteenth-century women poets.
Many, including Dickinson, used more than one strategy at the
same time.

Sometimes a formal strategy worked. Elizabeth Barrett
Browning mounted a raid upon the sonnet, successfully sexing
it female in her 'Sonnets from the Portuguese'. Her sonnet
sequence inspired generations of women sonnet-writers without

decreasing the long-term capacities of the form (in the short term the sonnet may have been somewhat feminized, as in the melancholy sonnets of the late nineteenth-century American poet Frederick Goddard Tuckerman). Dickinson too had a successful strategy, extending the lyric as a mode of knowledge, directing her effort unsentimentally to both female and universal issues – but Dickinson's kind of knowledge was not acceptable in her lifetime.

More often, however, appropriation was its own undoing since, when women poets took over a given genre or theme, it drifted towards a feminine social gendering. The idea of the beautiful was, like the idea of the feminine, associated in the nineteenth century with women but, as in Poe's 'The Philosophy of Composition', it was the beautiful woman as object of desire and not the woman writing about beauty who was being described.

In one of her most famous poems, Dickinson traces the movement of the idea of beauty across gender times. 'I died for Beauty', written shortly after Elizabeth Barrett Browning's death in 1861, presents Dickinson and Barrett Browning as companions:

> I died for Beauty – but was scarce
> Adjusted in the Tomb
> When One who died for Truth, was lain
> In an adjoining Room –

Together with her poem 'The Martyr Poets – did not tell –', these lines comprise Dickinson's homage to Barrett Browning's 'A Vision of Poets', in which her poet-knight hero has a vision in which he sees, grouped around an altar, the small company of poets 'royal with the truth',

> these were poets true,
> Who died for Beauty as martyrs do
> For Truth – the ends being scarcely two.

Barrett Browning's lines are in turn a Christianizing of the words on the urn in Keats's 'Ode to a Grecian Urn':

> 'Beauty is truth, truth beauty', — that is all
> Ye know on earth, and all ye need to know.

Although her poet hero was male, by writing 'A Vision of Poets' Elizabeth Barrett Browning made the equation of poetry—beauty—truth available to woman poets. Dickinson's 'I died for Beauty —' touches on this passage when she genders her second martyr-poet male: 'He questioned softly "Why I failed" '. The two poets are not lovers but 'brethren', 'Kinsmen'. Dickinson's gender shift would appear to register her consciousness of the borderline between tutorial sister-poet (Barrett Browning) and poet as type (Keats), who is male and historical.

Barrett Browning's very success stamped beauty as a feminine topic, with the weakness and lack of objectivity which that gendering implied. To some extent, her use of beauty was already retrograde in the 1840s. Keats had taken care to utter his Romantic credo through the voice of the urn; Barrett Browning identified Truth and Beauty in her own voice, while the medieval setting of 'A Vision of Poets' insulated her assertion from encounters with real life. Dickinson politely alludes to this problem in 'I died for Beauty' when, unusually, she admits the unexamined abstractions Beauty and Truth into her poem; if she is praising her heroine, she will not quibble about her heroine's conceptual terminology.

By the end of the nineteenth century, beauty was separated so radically from what Yeats called the 'grey Truth' of the present in his poem 'The Sad Shepherd' that he could imagine it only as part of a dream of a long-lost pastoral world. With Modernism, beauty survived, almost surreptitiously, in the work of women poets. In H.D., the beautiful is protected by her revisions of classical myth. In Marianne Moore it is couched in the specifics of object description. Louise Bogan found a middle way writing emotionally accurate poems in the Dickinson manner, but forming them into Swinburnesque lyrics. Talented American women poets like Edna St Vincent Millay and Elinor Wylie, who wrote 'fire and ice' lyrics about beauty and passion in traditional forms such as the emotive sonnet and the rhymed quatrain, have virtually disappeared from critical discourse.

Nor was symbolism exempt from a draining of power as it crossed gender lines. Many nineteenth-century women poets appear to have been unwilling to recognize that apparently neutral or feminine symbols such as the song-bird were in practice coded into narratives of the masculine, if for no other reason than that men had been writing the poems. Even before Blake's bird in 'How Sweet I Roamed', Keats's 'Ode to a Nightingale' and Shelley's 'To a Skylark', the song-bird had been the essential symbol of lyric flight. Blake's speaker is a male bird trapped by its sexuality; in Keats and Shelley the speaker hears a bird whose pure song makes him wish he too could transcend the physical.

As Cheryl Walker has noted in her extensive account in *The Nightingale's Burden*, many American poets took over the symbolic image of Philomela, the wounded nightingale-singer, mingling it with the Christian dove, which symbolized either the Holy Ghost or the soul. When the woman poet depicts herself as a bird (as Blake did), she runs the risk of reinforcing a received image of untutored 'natural' feminine singer. When she longs for the bird's incorporeal song, the absence of sexual difference between herself and the object of her desire can seem to trivialize her need.

In the English Book of Common Prayer, Psalm 55, verse 6, reads: 'O that I had wings like a dove; for then I would flee away, and be at rest.' The Lord tells those who have heard His word: 'Yet shall ye be as the wings of the dove; that is covered with silver wings, and her feathers like gold.' The popular English poet Felicia Hemans (1793–1835) who was widely read in the United States, echoed the Prayer Book while feminizing and sentimentalizing its spiritual longing in her poem:

> Oh! for thy wings, thou dove!
> Now sailing by with sunshine on thy breast;
> That, borne like thee above,
> I too might flee away, and be at rest!

For Hemans, it isn't sin or the limits of the physical but 'strong cords of love' and domestic obligation that pull her back hearthwards. In the American poet Elizabeth Oakes-Smith's 'An Incident', the occasion of finding an eagle's wing inspires the cry:

> O noble bird! why didst thou loose for me
> Thy eagle plume? Still unessayed, unknown
>   Must be that pathway fearless winged by thee;
> I ask it not, no lofty flight be mine,
>   I would not soar like thee, in loneliness to pine.

Like Hemans, Oakes-Smith locates the feminine in what is bound and socialized. The 'terror' she feels before the possibility of flight is the terror of isolation – the literal fate of any woman who took flight from home and family. In Kate Chopin's *The Awakening* such a flight is described, with death at the end of it.

Dickinson too depicted her imaginative self as a bird. Poems in which she combines this image with that of imprisonment, as in 'They Shut me up in Prose', have survived well, as has her incisive image of the poem inside the poet in 'Split the Lark – and you'll find the Music –'. Yet so powerful has been this century's revulsion against the association of poet and birdsong that many of her other bird poems now seem too sweet.

In fact, when Dickinson depicted natural objects, including birds, her accuracy of observation was worthy of a naturalist. Although she was certainly aware of the clichéd uses of bird imagery by other women, this seems if anything to have encouraged her to keep the image, but to investigate it her way. In the early 'For every Bird a Nest', written when she was still developing her characteristic imagery, she wrote:

> The Lark is not ashamed
> To build upon the ground
> Her modest house –
>
> Yet who of all the throng
> Dancing around the sun
> Does so rejoice?

Besides the lark, Dickinson describes the habits (and gives the names) of the bluebird, blue jay, bobolink, crow, hummingbird, oriole, owl, robin, sparrow, whippoorwill, woodpecker and wren. Her only dove is explicitly literary: Noah's dove. She doesn't mention the nightingale, a bird which is not found on the North American continent. The bird as type in the Dickinson poem is praised for its 'independent Ecstasy/Of Deity and Men' (in 'The Birds begun at Four o'clock −'). In 'To hear an Oriole sing', Dickinson makes it clear that only the bird itself determines 'whether it be Rune/Or whether it be none': the meaning of song belongs to the singer, not to 'The Fashion of the Ear'. If she ever so slightly longs to be the natural singer, Dickinson expresses that longing through the imagery of pleasure and work which informs her descriptions of her own poetry. In the late poem 'The Bird her punctual music brings', Dickinson concludes that:

> . . . Work might be electric Rest
> To those that Magic make −

In their balance of respect for the otherness of the natural object with recognition of a metaphoric drive towards meaning, Dickinson's compressions parallel Whitman's expansions in 'Out of the Cradle Endlessly Rocking'. Received culture, however, encourages different kinds of reading of the Whitman poem and the Dickinson group of poems. Whitman casts off his mantle of bardic confidence and identifies with a single 'he-bird', a 'singer solitary' who pours his life into song which only the boy hears; in context, this admission of isolation and smallness is deeply moving. Dickinson's birds cover a range of connotation and generally do not bear the burden of full identification, but our reading of them must struggle against the cultural assumption that a poem by a woman about a bird is necessarily sentimental.

Probably the most serious loss to poetry through the movement of themes across gender lines has been the imagery of the humble object. Such images are at the heart of Protestant meditative and poetic tradition, from early emblem books through the English and American poets of the seventeenth century, such as George Herbert, Anne Bradstreet and Edward Taylor. The poet is himself or herself a humble object, and the poem uses the imagery of everyday and domestic life to bring the experience of faith and doubt into a realistic context. Even when the struggle against doubt and the devil is depicted in heroic terms, as in John Bunyan's Puritan narrative *Grace Abounding*, it is acted out upon the stage of daily village life. This imagery survived into the Romantic period in such poems as William Blake's 'The Clod and the Pebble', but with the simultaneous development of Romantic heroism, it became almost an object of parody, rapidly losing its power to convey either the direct observation which animated Puritan writing, or any immediate access to belief.

With an irony which will now be familiar, it was at this point that the imagery of the humble object became prominent in women's poetry (or perhaps it should be said that it was at this point that many women began to get published, and they were attracted to the imagery of the humble object). The gender shift was far from complete; the poetry of John Clare and Walt Whitman has many evocations of humble natural objects. When used by women, however, the humble object served to enhance received cultural attitudes. Opportunities for modest subversion such as a description of the useful little acorn, were limited by the very smallness that excused them. In 'A Weed', Louise Chandler Moulton wrote:

> How shall a little weed grow,
> That has no sun?
> Rains fall and north winds blow, —
> What shall be done?

It is not just that the poem is weak, it sentimentalizes weakness to gain a place for the weak poet.

Emily Dickinson had this humble eye. In relation to Father or Master her humility was strategic, her smallness an often bitterly necessary ploy. In her more modest plays of proportion, as in her use of the word 'just', Dickinson engages in a small-scale subversion not dissimilar to that of poets in Griswold's anthology, *Female Poets of America*. Her tone, however, was not so much self-pity or special pleading as a bemused contempt. In her poems of massive proportion-play, such as 'Safe in their Alabaster Chambers −', her contempt becomes sublime.

In Dickinson's poetry of observation, any object will suffice, though she prefers the close focus of the singular: 'a hay', a weed, grass stubble, the gentian, the dandelion, the daisy. Always she respects the separate life of the object, even when she extracts meanings from it to set in her metaphoric diadem. When Dickinson connects observation to feeling, her life is the singular material she had ready to hand. While the 'I' that explores the experience of loss or anguish or passion draws directly upon the experiences of Emily Dickinson, once those experiences are in the poem, the poem goes to great lengths to block references back to the biographical situation. The specificity of Dickinson's speaker is consistent only in its female sex (the one per cent or so of Dickinson's poems which have a male speaker leap up from the rest of her work as exceptions).

The perennial objection to the first-person lyric is that it is limited by the emotional experience of the writer who is speaking. It could also be said that all writing is similarly limited. When Dickinson wrote to Higginson that the speaker in her poems was 'not . . . me − but a supposed person' (*Letters*, II, p. 412), she was, I think, trying to describe her adaptation of her 'I' (or 'she' or 'it' or absent speaker) to the immediate poetic situation. Not that her poems were spoken by dramatic characters or personae (though there are a few personae-poems), but that the 'I' is the investigative instrument. In the absence of Dickinson as a consistent modern influence, poets of this century have had to recover the poetry of the humble object from earlier sources − if they have wanted to recover it at all.

When Elizabeth Bishop sought to recover the humble gaze, she looked back beyond Dickinson to George Herbert, particularly 'Love Unknown', his poem of self-dissection. Bishop's poem 'Sandpiper', about a small bird, traces this movement back and forward. The sandpiper, running obsessively along the beach, is 'a student of Blake';[10] like Blake in 'Auguries of Innocence', he is seeing 'the world in a grain of sand'. Blake wrote in a prophetic, bardic voice, while Bishop writes so modestly that her poem has no speaker and, seemingly, no objective beyond observing the sandpiper. In the poem's conclusion,

> he is preoccupied,
> looking for something, something, something
> Poor bird, he is obsessed!
> The millions of grains are black, white, tan and gray,
> mixed with quartz grains, rose and amethyst.

The furthest source for this imagery is the Book of Revelations. If Bishop is looked at in the light of Dickinson, we can more easily see a line of humility, revelation and detail running from the Renaissance to the present day.

CHAPTER NINE

WHAT EMILY KNEW

To fill a Gap
Insert the Thing that caused it –
  ('To fill a Gap')

To relieve the irreparable degrades it.
  (Letter to Maria Whitney, 1878, *Letters*, II, p. 602)

We do not require a restructured theory of literary history to enjoy Emily Dickinson's poetry. But what Emily knew – what Dickinson found out about and wrote about – raises the issue of the historical path or paths which lead to future writing. Partly through historical summary, partly through a more detailed analysis of the role played by sublimation in nineteenth- and twentieth-century theories of creativity, a new path for Dickinson's knowledge can be traced.

Dickinson's difference within American tradition may best be seen by setting her work opposite the Orphic line of American poetry – that bardic, prophetic line of the poet-priest which Allen Ginsberg has called the only true tradition, beginning (in his expansive listing) with Biblical 'structures, psalms & lamentations' and proceeding eccentrically forward through English poetry via Christopher Smart, William Blake and Shelley to Melville, Whitman, Hart Crane's 'Atlantis' and thence to Ginsberg himself. As for other poetry, Ginsberg declares: 'The only poetic tradition is the Voice out of the burning bush. The rest is trash & will be consumed.'[1]

Although Orphic vocation need not necessarily predicate a unitary view of life, in American practice it has done so, with

Emerson describing an Orphic poet in 'The Poet', while setting
out a holistic world view which his ideal poet is said to hold. In
the holistic line of American poetry, established by Emerson
and Whitman, dualism of mind−body or self−other is quite
deliberately not admitted, as a threat to poetic knowledge.
When it is described at all, dualism is declared conquered.
Emerson declares he can see everything through his 'transparent eyeball'. Whitman extends his nakedness erotically into
nature and other people. The paralysis felt by a Romantic like
Coleridge in the face of a fixed and dead exterior nature has
been asserted away. Every holistic poem aspires to be a version of Whitman's 'The Song of the Answerer'. It is not a
poetry of questions, yet when questions arise, they are all
the more dangerous because the apparatus for inquiry and
doubt has been discarded. When nature suddenly looks 'other',
the holistic poet may stand baffled, like Whitman in his
dark poem, 'Of the Terrible Doubt of Appearances'. In
Whitman's 'As I Ebb'd with the Ocean of Life', a second self
'jeers' with 'mock-congratulatory signs and bows' at the
poet who cannot begin to understand the world he pretends
to describe.

> I perceive I have not really understood any thing, not
>   a single object, and that no man ever can,
> Nature here in sight of the sea taking advantage of me
>   to dart upon me and sting me,
> Because I have dared to open my mouth to sing at all.

For the holistic poet, danger arises from the problematic
status of poetic power itself and the conflicts which that power
may generate. As the holistic poet approximates his life to his
self-definition as poet, his own personal flaws may seem to seep
into his work and render it vicious, obscene or incoherent −
though still demonically powerful. This danger pervades Hart
Crane's lyrics and finds its classic though somewhat tongue-in-
cheek expression in Whitman's 'Whoever You Are Holding Me
Now in Hand' from 'Calamus': 'Nor will my poems do good
only, they will do just as much evil, perhaps more'. If person
and poem remain separate, the poem's unrealized being can

then behave like a demonic epipsychidion or soul-companion, turning on the poet, wounding and mocking him.

The holistic vision is one response to the problem of the other, a problem which philosophic idealism had made central to mid nineteenth-century thought. Dickinson is obviously not a holistic poet, but she is not strictly dualistic either. Natural objects and phenomena are seen as living and yielding up meaning without strain. However, to the extent that the 'I' in her poetry represents an empirical self, a woman living in the world, that 'I' is put in danger when it relates to others. Dickinson never resolved the status of the other in her life. The combination of this anguish and her scrupulous heuristic push means that her poems never presume unduly on the inner life of others, never lose respect for the otherness of the sources of her metaphors.

Within a poem, Dickinson rarely doubts her own power. Nor does she consider her power to be actually or potentially evil. She hates false speech, usually oral, and what she calls in 'The Leaves like Women interchange' the 'Exclusive Confidence' of gossip. But the truth available to writing and the drive of thought aren't doubted. The mocking rebarbative split self of Whitman's 'As I Ebb'd With the Ocean of Life' is absent from Dickinson. Instead, as she writes in 'I reckon — when I count at all —' poets 'Comprehend the Whole' so that 'Their Summer — lasts a Solid Year —'.

Outside the realm of the heuristic, in what Dickinson called the 'magic prison' of everyday life in the bitter poem 'Of God we ask one favor', the proportions can and do go wrong. Power is blocked by circumstance, and trapped repetition is substituted for discovery. Patriarchal society and the power-laden speech of Dickinson's poetry of knowledge are at odds. Where poetry must be figured forth by the person of the poet, that person suffers: 'Civilization — spurns — the Leopard!/Was the Leopard — bold?'

Dickinson's 'I' feels epistemological desire, and that desire is fulfilled in the pleasure of the poem's arc: as in the Orphic tradition, self, vocation and powerful expression are inseparable. Dickinson sounds the Orphic note when she crowns herself queen, only to turn to other facets of her desired poetic self by her consistent modesty, her profoundly non-bardic address to the question at hand, her turning away from identification with audience. Reading also is a satisfiable desire: in 'Unto my Books − so good to turn −', books 'Enamor − in Prospective −/And satisfy − obtained −'.

It may be possible to say with some truth that much poetry is about knowledge, and Dickinson's poetry quintessentially so, but it would be most unwise to declare the same about life. Those desires of the person which are not epistemological point to the special Dickinsonian 'other', that which desires and fails.

For Wallace Stevens in 'Notes Towards a Supreme Fiction', 'not to have is the beginning of desire' ('It Must be Abstract', II); the poem's object of desire readily transposes itself into the metaphysical 'what is not', which is unattainable by token of being unavailable to experience. In Stevens this recognition is oddly soothing, since while it will never go away, it is also not one's immediate responsibility to solve it. For Dickinson it is the empirical, everyday woman in the world who desires both what she is not, and what is not, knowing that these desires are unfulfillable: 'Heaven − is what I cannot reach!' This is the root case of irony: the constantly re-opened, constantly experienced break between desire and desired.

Stevens temporarily solves the dilemma of desire in 'Notes Towards a Supreme Fiction' by having desire imitate the natural cycle of the seasons. By desiring something else, the mind recognises that what it already has 'is not'. Negation of the present precipitates the future; desire makes for proper time and order. For the living self whom Dickinson brings into her poems as her instrument, desiring is continual and innate, a state of being that defines being itself. In poetry, the consequence is an intimate command; in the experience of others, it is disaster:

> The heart asks Pleasure − first −
> And then − Excuse from Pain −
> And then − those little Anodynes
> That deaden suffering −

There's no future of assuaged desire because the denial of fulfilment negates futures. Dickinson's stunned self is tilted out of time.

The question of being bears directly upon Dickinson's poetry by providing its major referent, the 'I' who is the woman, who suffers, who is 'there'. Dickinson's poems are insistent encounters of power with that otherness 'that scalds me now – that scalds me now!', as Dickinson writes at the end of 'I shall know why – when Time is over –'. Major recognitions do come out of knowing pain, but they are not imitative exclamations of pain. The notable calm of many Dickinson poems on searing or anguished topics arises from investigative command of what the issue entails: 'It was not Death, for I stood up'. In the poems of the years 1861–3 the pattern of painful investigation is so pronounced as to constitute a mannerism. Even the crossing from life to death fascinates this heuristic poet as a manifestation of otherness worthy of intense inquiry.

When Dickinson allowed knowledge to the poet and poem but meditated on the enforced split between these two and the empirical, social self, she addressed one of the obsessions of twentieth-century criticism. Much of this century's critical literature in English has been devoted to separating empirical self from poetic persona, an effort which has followed the apparent lead given by the poets Yeats, Eliot and Pound, each of whom, for different reasons, employed personae to create non-biographical speakers. It is important, then, to reconsider the Dickinson 'I' and see what split, if any, there is between the feeling self and the writing poet. For this we must look beyond American literary history to psychology and epistemology.

One of my purposes has been to institute the way Dickinson 'knows' as a major answer within what is by now an almost two-hundred-year-old debate on the relation of the artist to the art work. In philosophical terms, much of Dickinson's achievement is on the boundary between the ontology (theory of being) and the epistemology (theory of knowledge) of the poem. This boundary has been most brilliantly defined in recent years by Paul de Man in his collection *Blindness and Insight*.[2]

In his essay 'The Sublimation of the Self', de Man develops the argument (first advanced by the Swiss psychoanalyst Ludwig Binswanger) that 'the plenitude of the [artistic] work stems from a reduction of the self' (p. 41). Although he discusses this phenomenon of plenitude and reduction in absolute terms, he is in fact carrying out a critique of uses of the idealist inheritance, an area very close to Dickinson's operations. Since the Romantic period, a lessening or distorting of full human self in order to serve art has indeed often been the case, with Whitman and Dickinson providing notable exceptions. It is one of the central themes of twentieth-century Modernist writing, and was also close to the way many avant-gardist writers and artists depicted artists' lives: Proust's Marcel, Joyce's Stephen Daedalus, Thomas Mann's Tonio Kröger and Dr Faustus. This pattern of inner and outer exile has a nineteenth-century origin in the lives of Flaubert, Ibsen, Baudelaire, Wagner. It forms a bridge between romantic and modern ideas of artistic selfhood.

According to de Man, this purportedly necessary sublimation of self involves loss; there is quite literally a lessening of those parts of the person which would enable him to live with any felicity in the world. In the case of Ibsen, for example, the sacrifices and renunciations required of the artist are shown not to be a kind of trading upwards, in which false bourgeois virtues are exchanged for new, higher, creative ones. On the contrary, 'in the process the self is stripped of eminently concrete and legitimate attributes and is exposed at once to more insidious forms of inauthenticity' (p. 42). The finished work owes its objectivity to a particular kind of subjectivity by which the artist strips himself of everything which is not self, generating a kind of goal-orientated, inauthentic solipsism of self as self.

Dickinson envisaged a personal self which has various operations: in its acts of thought and writing it has knowledge and power; in its social and emotive acts it has knowledge, but its view of its own power and the power itself vary wildly.

At no point, however, does Dickinson describe or accept a sublimation of herself in the service of art. The self may well fail in its human aspirations and passions, and it suffers while failing, but it is not art or the choice of artistic vocation which inflicts this wound. Instead, art is a way by which life can be lived, either directly or by other means.

Dickinson's view of art as a positive mode of being is consistent with attitudes about the relation of experience to art in a number of other nineteenth-century women writers. Writers such as George Sand, George Eliot, Elizabeth Barrett Browning and Christina Rossetti saw their talent as a way by which they could live fuller lives; except for Rossetti, these were also writers Dickinson read and admired. Gender difference is not the only way to discuss alternatives to the distortion of one's human role, but it does seem as if the different social choices open to women in the nineteenth century profoundly affected their views about the relation of self to art, encouraging them to see the benefits of creativity in a way which is so positive it verges upon the sentimental. This generally shared view did not, however, lead to a shared concept of self within the work, or of the kinds of knowledge which that poetic self could have; there is scant common denominator there.

Dickinson's relation to the post-Romantic model of sublimated artistic self may best be seen in the poem in which she most nearly approximates it, 'My Life had stood — a Loaded Gun'. This poem, much anthologized today because of its phallic imagery, is a definition of self as pure artistic agency. Once having been 'identified' by a beloved preceptor-figure or 'Owner', the speaker is 'carried . . . away' like a bride, a pet or a purchase. A number of Dickinson poems testify to her pleasure at being 'named', at having the linguistically magical power of an appropriate title conferred upon her: 'You said that I "was great" — One Day —', one such poem begins.

The linguistic betrothal sweeps away both the 'life' and its new owner, taking them out of society and into a separate, independent, green world, which is significantly not pastoral but associated with freedom and power — 'Sovereign':

And now We roam in Sovereign Woods —
And now We hunt the Doe —
And every time I speak for Him —
The Mountains straight reply —

Temporality shifts from pluperfect ('had stood') to past ('passed — identified') to a continuously reiterating present of 'now'. The new power is not a gift from the owner; his role has been to release an already existing power; thereafter 'I speak for Him' while he stays silent. The significance could be that she does the speaking or that her 'speech is deathly because she is the agent of her patriarchal master'. The thrill, however, is unmistakable. The 'I' is now fully identified with the life of pure destructive power; she is what she does, and the mountains echo back their correspondent rifle-crack.

What is radical about this poem is not the fact that a female poet is describing herself, consciously or unconsciously, in phallic terms. Dickinson is consistently lucid about power. The passage does indeed have an element of sublime parody, but this had to do with Dickinson's note that to be a gun is to be only a gun: the phallic is pure instrumentality. When she wishes to talk about more complex kinds of power the imagery shifts to the volcano or the witch.

The gun temporarily 'is' the life. An etymological palindrome may explain: my expression expresses me, speech presses the 'me' out into the open. The speaking 'I' is thus feminine, masculine, an object and an animal — all sexes and none, a commanding voice for the expression of knowledge. In a nineteenth-century context it is also notable for its eschewing of analogies with the divine.

To say that Dickinson is alert to sexual personae in her poetry is to understate the case. Shifts of pronouns in her work change the entire perspective from which a metaphor or poem is written. Since emotive desire and its rebuffs arise directly out of Dickinson's situation as a woman, and she chooses to represent those situations undistanced in her poetry, a female 'I' carrying all the personal implications of womanhood directs the poem's knowing unless Dickinson specifically designates

otherwise. The sexually multivalent 'I' of 'My life had stood
. . .' exhibits male, female and object-like characteristics,
making it everything and nothing.

However loudly it resonates, that gun (like the bird of 'They
shut me up in Prose') is merely a metaphoric engine. When
Dickinson wishes to convey other aspects of artistic agency, she
changes metaphor. The next stanza describes the pleasures of
exploding:

> And do I smile, such cordial light
> Upon the Valley glow —
> It is as a Vesuvian face
> Had let its pleasure through —

Volcanoes — expressed by the representative metonym of
Vesuvius — fulfil themselves by exploding: exploding is what
they have been created to do. There are implications of female
sexual pleasure in 'smile', 'glow', and 'let its pleasure through',
as if the exploding volcano is also a sun whose light is burst-
ing through clouds. This flow is a highly visible oxymoronic
fire-flood.

The speaker's pleasure-in-agency is carefully distinguished
from male—female sexual relationship, even when such a
meaning could have readily been disguised. Dickinson wishes
to exclude even the slightest hint that artistic agency is a
metaphor for human companionship; agency isn't 'sharing'.
Also, guns are for firing. Together master and agent shoot
down the doe, the merely feminine.

> And when at Night — Our good Day done —
> I guard my Master's Head —
> 'Tis better than the Eider-Duck's
> Deep Pillow — to have shared —

In the primitive world of agency, the enemies of her friend are
her enemies:

> To foe of His — I'm deadly foe —
> None stir the second time —
> On whom I lay a Yellow Eye —
> Or an emphatic Thumb —

The Orphic way is to restrain from murder of any kind. In the hands of Whitman, Orphism is a masculine polymorphism. But this is not the Orphic way. It is a female heuristic murderousness. If the violent discharge of that which has been 'loaded' inside her makes her be male and female, perhaps a supernatural agency is after all at work, but it is not a Christian one.

Dickinson's 'I' is a witch, and not for the only time in her verse. The power of poetic agency is beyond Christian rules of good and evil; when what you want to kill has been killed, it is 'Our good Day done −'. The absence of Whitmanesque or Wordsworthian awe at the poetic assignment is striking. Dickinson is matter-of fact about her fate.

The last quatrain looks outside the poem's earlier metaphoric terms of reference:

> Though I than He − may longer live
> He longer must − than I −
> For I have but the power to kill
> Without − the power to die −

The powerfully argued paradox forces a new frame of reference upon the poem. In life, 'I' may outlive my mentor but, as the terms shift, it is both ontologically and poetically necessary for him to outlive me, if the primacy of the human over pure agency is to be maintained. The 'must' gives way, however, as the argument closes over it; the reason for this need for the master's life is that Dickinson knows she is immortal. In her mid-thirties when she wrote this poem, virtually unpublished and unpublishable, she already knew that as a poet she no longer had the option of dying. As Yeats recognized in 'Sailing to Byzantium', the poet as pure poem-machine never dies.

In the model of creativity that de Man criticizes, the artist sublimates his life to his art; he substitutes the one for the other. Both art and artist bear marks of this inner wounding, which can cause the artist to feel the sickening sense 'of ascending beyond his own limits into a place from which he can no longer descend' (p. 47). The place to look for such symptoms in Dickinson would be in her many poems of anguish and loss.

Not surprisingly, there are no poems depicting artistic over-reaching and a consequent fall. In life, however, Dickinson often over-reached: the characteristic anguish of her poems arises from her wilful refusal to sublimate. The speaker 'knows' the consequence of her need or passion, but she lets it happen.

Dickinson's anguish and its successor, numb despair, arise from a desire which is empirical:

> 'I want' — it pleaded — All its life —
> I want — was chief it said

The self 'wants', desiring what it lacks. A brilliant and little-known poem exposes the operation of this human need:

> To fill a Gap
> Insert the Thing that caused it —
> Block it up
> With Other — and 'twill yawn the more —
> You cannot solder an Abyss
> With Air.

The poem vehemently rejects sublimation. Desire requires its original object, that which incited it; desire is not transferable. The sexual implication of 'Gap' and 'Insert the Thing' point to the physical goal of most human desire. Or the gap may have opened long before, in childhood; whatever its referent, it yawns now. Dickinson's abstract terms 'Other' and 'Abyss' and the homely actions 'Block it up' and 'solder' locate the missing body between them. Knowledgeable about such loss, Dickinson instructs us: if you try a substitute, whether physical or metaphysical, you make a grotesque category mistake.

If the gap is not filled, and it is not, the next stage is despair, the emotion in Dickinson which most closely approximates death.

> There is a pain — so utter —
> It swallows substance up —
> Then covers the Abyss with Trance —
> So Memory can step
> Around — across — upon it —

Pain devours what must once have been the body, then ob-
scures its work by building a trance-like bridge or skin for the
personified Memory. This superficially healing repression
actually condemns the consciousness to eternal 'swoon' as the
alternative to dropping 'Bone by Bone' with open eyes into the
abyss of despair.

Other poems display other facets of this state — 'After great
pain, a formal feeling comes —' and 'I felt a Funeral, in
my brain' are chilling chronicles of psychic 'fall'. Yet even
when depicting conditions of extreme anguish, Dickinson's
pressure is towards a precise knowledge which only language
can give.

It was Freud's wisdom in *Civilization and its Discontents* to
accept an inevitable sublimation of original desire as the price
of civilization. In the refinement of this wisdom, art is the
product of the reductive sublimation of the artist's human self.
Dickinson's wisdom is not to substitute but to keep desiring,
not to develop a special poet-self but to use language to
understand what happens to the human self.

In 'The Sublimation of Self' Paul de Man dealt incisively
and humanely with the poetic type of the over-reacher. Dickinson offers an alternative type of the poet. Her method was
painful to her, in the time, the place and the family where she
lived; but if offers an instance of bravery to us. She addressed
herself to knowledge, one or two complex truths in each poem.
She did not consider that one could over-reach truth, or that
the specific truths she saw were beyond language. The 'use' of
her poems is in what they discover, as they give themselves
over to knowing. They are in that sense truly private, no
matter where they are published.

The absence of 'use' in Dickinson generates one more question, that of her poems' presentation to the reader. When
Emily Dickinson realized that neither Higginson nor Bowles
nor anyone else she was likely to meet was going to understand
what she was writing, she departed permanently from the
exchange economy of literature. After that all her poems were
gifts. Sometimes Dickinson sent flowers with her letters,
sometimes poems; at other times she sent poems but called

them flowers. Her booklets of poems function as bouquets, each bunch or all the poems making a kind of diadem of metaphors encircling the meaning which the metaphors themselves generate. In life, she sent some poems as love-tokens. Now they survive as unaddressed gifts.

NOTES

Introduction

1. The three-volume *The Poems of Emily Dickinson*, edited by Thomas H. Johnson, Cambridge, Mass.: The Belknap Press of Harvard University Press, 1955 was the first complete scholarly edition, and the first to print Dickinson's poems with her punctuation and capitalization intact. The most readily available complete Dickinson is a one-volume edition of Johnson's collection, *The Complete Poems of Emily Dickinson*, Faber & Faber, 1975 (this edition does not include variorum versions). Unless otherwise indicated, all quotations are from the one-volume edition.

2. *The Letters of Emily Dickinson*, edited by Thomas H. Johnson and Theodora Ward, Cambridge, Mass.: The Belknap Press of Harvard University Press, 1958, hereafter referred to as *Letters*.

3. David Porter, *Dickinson: The Modern Idiom*, p. 1. Porter's study and this one share a view of Dickinson as 'different', but see varying consequences of that difference.

4. Vincent B. Leitch, in *Deconstructive Criticism: An Advanced Introduction*, Hutchinson, London, 1983, quotes approvingly an attack by Joseph Riddell:

   Yale deconstruction preserves and recanonizes the great writers, works, and tradition. . . . As far as Riddell is concerned, the Yale deconstructors either deny, as do [Geoffrey] Hartman and [Harold] Bloom, or tame, as do [Paul] de Man and [Hillis] Miller, *écriture* [writing]. They privilege *literary* language and texts. They keep the author as genius alive. They preserve the great tradition undisturbed. They delimit interpretation. Curiously, they imply that literature is complete and that we do not need more texts. This latter notion seems oddly strucuralist in its synchronic or spatial reduction of literary history.

   (p. 96)

Toril Moi, in Chapter 2 of her recent *Sexual/Textual Politics*, Methuen, London, 1985, suggests that American feminist critics have, perhaps inadvertently, been recapitulating this privileging in their treatment of female tradition.

5. 'In symbolizing one situation by means of another, metaphor "infuses" the feelings attached to the symbolizing situation into the heart of the situation that is symbolized', Paul Ricoeur, *The Rule of Metaphor*, p. 190. Ricoeur's Study 6, on the role of resemblance in metaphor, is a meticulous and thoughful analysis of theories of how figurative language achieves meaning.

Chapter One: Dickinson and Knowledge

1. For a perceptive treatment of Dickinson's understanding of the problem of other minds, see Christopher Benfey's *Emily Dickinson and the Problem of Others*. Benfey's book is a useful antidote to remarks about Dickinson's purportedly excessive subjectivity.

2. For a different view of the same phenomenon, see Susan R. Van Dyne's article, 'Double Monologues: Voices in American Women's Poetry', *Massachusetts Review*, XXII, 3 (Autumn, 1982), pp. 461–85. Van Dyne's thesis is that women's poetry is characterized by a double consciousness. This doubling is not one imposed by social readings of gender, as Sandra Gilbert and Susan Gubar argue in *The Madwoman in the Attic*. Rather 'the split itself, the inherent doubleness of perspective of tone' (p. 464) has to do with the women poets standing 'beside themselves'. She discusses 'Dickinson's speaker standing watchfully by her subjective self in order to examine the dimensions and co-habitants of her chamber of consciousness'. (p. 465)

3. My discussion is based on Derrida's *Writing and Difference* and *Of Grammatology*.

4. See George Whicher, *This Was a Poet: A Critical Biography of Emily Dickinson*, pp. 107–8.

5. See Rebecca Patterson, *The Riddle of Emily Dickinson*, p. 384.

6. Some support for a literary reading can be found in mid-nineteenth-century American critical terminology, where 'jewel' and 'paste' were used to mean good and bad art (implying that 'bad' art is not a separate type but, like kitsch, a parodic imitation of good art). In *The United States Magazine and Democratic Review*, 17 July 1845, pp. 63–5, a reviewer attacked amateur critics for not being capable of distinguishing between 'false wares' by

fellow amateurs and true professional literature. The amateur praises equally 'the jewel and the mock paste', while the true critic presumably sets up the canon. Quoted in Michael T. Gilmore, *American Romanticism and the Marketplace*, pp. 55–6.

7. Dickinson's relation to Shakespeare has not yet received adequate treatment. The most thorough study of her language is Brita Lindburg-Seyersted's *The Voice of the Poet*.

8. The fullest account of Dickinson's imagery of circumference is found in Jane Donahue Eberwein's *Dickinson: Strategies of Limitation*, Amherst, Mass., University of Massachusetts Press, 1985, which sees circumference as the infinite alternative to Dickinson's exaggerated sense of limitation. Eberwein offers a valuable discussion of Dickinson's sense of death as limit.

Chapter Two: Dickinson and Difference

1. One notable instance is Nina Baym's analysis of the structuring of women's narrative in her excellent *Women's Fiction: a Guide to Novels by and about Women in America 1820–1870*. Tillie Olsen's *Silences*, Virago Press, 1980, offers a compassionate understanding of how the conditions of a writer's life determine what kind of writing, if any, he or she can produce. Cheryl Walker's *The Nightingale's Burden* puts poets such as Dickinson and Anne Bradstreet in a larger context of American women's poetry.

2. This tendency is more true of the French theorists such as Derrida, Julia Kristeva and Michel Foucault and the radical 'schizoanalysis' of Gilles Deleuze and Felix Guattari. With the exception of Joseph Riddell, it is markedly less true of American deconstruction (see Introduction, note 4).

3. Dickinson replied to Thomas Wentworth Higginson's 'Letter to a Young Contributor' in the April 1862 *Atlantic Monthly*. When Higginson wrote back asking Dickinson's age, experience and education, she answered that 'I made no verse – but one or two – until this winter – Sir –.' In fact she had written about 350 poems. She wrote that she 'went to school – but in your manner of the phrase – had no education', when she had had a year in college. For reading, she dutifully mentioned writers whom Higginson had mentioned in his article, though the Brownings and Revelations do appear (*Letters*, II, p. 404).

4. George Whicher, *This Was a Poet: A Critical Biography of Emily Dickinson* appeared in 1938, and Allen Tate's laudatory essay

'Emily Dickinson' was first printed in 1932 (reprinted in Richard Sewall, ed., *Emily Dickinson: A Collection of Critical Essays*).

5. I am grateful to Professor Robert Gross of Amherst College for pointing out how Dickinson's literary practice remained consistently appropriate to the genteel manners of her class.

6. *Sister Outsider: Essays and Speeches*, Trumansburg, New York, The Crossing Press, 1984, p. 45. See also Lord's essay 'Age, Race, Class and Sex; Women Redefining Difference' in the same collection, pp. 114–23.

7. Adrienne Rich, *Of Woman Born*, p. 16.

Chapter Three: The House of the Father

1. George S. Merriam, *The Life and Times of Samuel Bowles*, New York, The Century Co., 1885, I p. 9.

2. Emily Dickinson was following national politics closely at this time. She joked that she should have been a representative at the Whig Convention, if only to visit Sue Gilbert, who was then living in Baltimore: 'Why cant *I* be a Delegate to the great Whig Convention? – dont I know all about Daniel Webster, and the Tariff, and the Law? Then, Susie I could see you, during a pause in the session – but I dont like this country at all, and I shant stay here any longer! 'Delenda est' America, Massachusetts and all!' (*Letters*, I, p. 212). Was she quoting the Latin phrase used to describe the destruction of Carthage because she considered the United States ruined by the slavery compromises? Eminent as Edward Dickinson was locally, he is not mentioned once in George Lowell Austin's *The History of Massachusetts from the Landing of the Pilgrims to the Present Time*, Boston, B. B. Russell, Estes & Lauriat, 1876.

3. Shira Wolosky, *Emily Dickinson: a Voice of War*. Wolosky also argues that the heightened emotional tone of Dickinson's poetry during the war years may be partially indebted to the fervour of the time.

4. Within a family it is difficult to mark the line where loving compliance ends and submission begins. When Higginson invited Dickinson to visit him in Boston (a convenient train ride away), she felt she must decline: 'I had promised to visit my Physician for a few days in May, but Father objects because he is in the habit of me' (*Letters*, II, p. 450). Lavinia did travel.

5. Samuel Bowles, covering the Unitarian National Convention in

1863, wrote that 'In the discussions, especially on the last day, there was manifest the old effort, ever recurring, to get on God's side of the universe, and see the Infinite through finite eyes. . . . Perhaps those who attempted it thought they succeeded, but it cannot be done, and all inferences from what men suppose they see on that side are phantasms and fallacies' (Merriam, I, p. 401). Bowles was a Unitarian himself, so he may have discussed such a pragmatic theology with Emily Dickinson.

Chapter Four: The Spoken and the Written

1. Sewall argues for parallels between Dickinson's and Taylor's religious imagery; Sewall, II, pp. 709–10.
2. Sewall, II, p. 566 Higginson's immediate reaction to meeting Dickinson was more favourable than his later, considered view; although his wife had not met Dickinson, he came to agree with her hostile opinion. See also *Letters*, II, pp. 473–6.
3. Jay Leydya, *The Years and Hours of Emily Dickinson*, II, p. 237. This letter is quoted in Sandra Gilbert's article about Dickinson's self-symbolization, 'The Wayward Nun beneath the Hill: Emily Dickinson and the Mysteries of Womanhood', in Suzanne Juhasz, ed., *Feminist Critics Read Emily Dickinson*, pp. 22–44. Accounts of Mabel Loomis Todd's role in creating, selling and moderating the Dickinson myth can be found in Sewall, I, pp. 215–28 and *passim*, and in Polly Longworth's *Austin and Mabel: the Amherst Love Affair and Love Letters of Austin Dickinson and Mabel Loomis Todd*.
4. Longworth, p. 3.
5. Fuller accounts of middle-class feminine activity can be found in Ann Douglas, *The Feminization of American Culture*.
6. George Eliot, *The Legend of Jubal and Other Poems*, Edinburgh and London, Wm. Blackwood and Sons, 1874, p. 56.
7. One of Nathaniel Hawthorne's central concerns was the expiation of guilt for these crimes of the patriarchs. In *The Scarlet Letter* Hawthorne divides up womanhood in a noble – but still all too familiar – exploitation of clichéd gender divisions. He boldly claims 'good' female qualities for the creative, passionate and undoubtedly dangerous Hester Prynne. However, he deflects 'bad' female qualities onto another woman, who is old, ugly and unmarried: Mistress Hibbins. Mistress Hibbins is a witch who, Hawthorne assures us, was later burnt at the stake.

8. Leydya, II, p. 237.

9. Nineteenth-century rhetoric texts were particularly stultifying because they continued the seventeenth- and eighteenth-century practice of combining Ciceronian rhetoric (political oratory) with the principles of Aristotle's *Poetics*, which was an analysis of dramatic poetry. Much remains to be discovered about Dickinson's extensive use of classical rhetorical tropes. I certainly think her work has many etymological and macaronic puns; this would be a powerful way of simultaneously writing 'slant' and delving into the individual word (rather than beyond it). Important arguments for the influence of Latin prosody and rhetoric on Dickinson's poetry have been set forth by Lois Cuddy in 'The Influence of Latin Poetics on Emily Dickinson's Style', *Comparative Literature Studies*, XIII (1976), pp. 214–29, and in 'The Latin Imprint on Emily Dickinson's Poetry: Theory and Practice', *American Literature* 50 (1978–9), pp. 74–84.

10. Robert N. Hudspeth, ed., *The Letters of Margaret Fuller*, Vol. I *1817–38*, Vol. II *1839–41*, Ithaca and London, Cornell University Press, 1983, I, pp. 195–6. The preacher in question was not the famous Unitarian minister Dr. Channing, but his nephew, William Henry Channing, who was later (1852) to co-edit a memoir of Fuller.

11. See Gerda Lerner, *The Majority Finds its Past: Placing Women in History*, for accounts of the beginnings of the American women's movement, particularly in connection with black women. Lerner's biography, *The Grimké Sisters from South Carolina*, New York, Schocken, 1971, describes their public speaking in depth. The selections in Chapters 3, 4 and 5 of *Root of Bitterness*, edited by Nancy F. Cott, New York, Sutton, 1972, offer a good picture of women's status at mid-century. In Carol Hymowitz and Michaele Weissman's *A History of Women in America* is a condensed but very informative account of the origins of the women's movement, particularly in relation to meetings and speeches.

12. Hudspeth, ed., *The Letters of Margaret Fuller*, II, p. 87.

13. Ralph Waldo Emerson, *Essays and Lectures*, edited by Joel Porte, New York, Library of America, 1983, p. 104.

14. *Springfield Republican*, 19 May 1886. The obituary was unsigned.

15. Derrida argues that from Plato to Heidegger, all philosophers have excluded writing from their consideration of the sign. Whether or not this has actually been the case, it is not felt by

Dickinson, who does not find writing suffering from an exclusion, though she vigorously attacks what Derrida would call 'logocentric' or 'phonocentric' theories of meaning. There are other differences, mainly along the plane of what is 'before' and what is 'after'. For Derrida things are not only dispersed, they are deferred, delayed, by the recognition of difference; while for Dickinson the thing is always real in the present. Also Derrida stresses that his 'difference' is an origin, while Dickinson has little interest in theories of origin.

16. *Writing and Difference*, p. 197. Derrida interestingly wonders if Western 'logo-phonocentrism' has come to its historical limit; Freud then receives credit as beginning the end of 'the history of the possibility of symbolism *in general*'.

17. While Derrida is advancing an argument about transcendence, his vocabulary of 'egoity', 'egological life' and 'my living present' is that of a traditionally male-gendered subject ('Violence and Metaphysics', *Writing and Difference*. In this context see Luce Irigaray, 'Any Theory of the "Subject" has always been appropriated by the "Masculine" ' in *The Speculum of Other Women*, pp. 133–46. Derrida assumes the existence of an 'ego in general' or 'subjective *a priori*'. The existence of God, he writes, does not depend 'upon me', but 'God's divinity (the infinite alterity of the infinite other, for example) must have a meaning for the ego in general' (p. 132). Dickinson is, of course, acutely aware of the otherness of God, but it is doubtful whether she would write that God would not have a meaning except for that ascribed to Him. She writes more pragmatically, in a historical situation in which God already had a meaning, and her speaker is more given over to its topic than an 'ego in general' might be likely to be.

Chapter Five: A Woman Writing Herself

1. Emerson then remarked, in a famous pithy phrase, 'Instead of Man Thinking, we have the bookworm. Hence, the book-learned class, who value books, as such', *Essays and Lectures*, p. 57.
2. See Sandra Gilbert and Susan Gubar, *The Madwoman in the Attic*.
3. In context, 'Before I got my Eye put out' refers to gender. Out of context, it is about the situation of having to choose between a wrongly formulated kind of sight and blindness. In 'When the Soul Selects: Emily Dickinson's Attack on New England Symbolism', *American Literature* 51 (1979–80), pp. 349–63, E. Miller

Budick makes a strong case for the blindness coming from the Puritan inheritance of spiritually acquisitive sight.

4. *Standard Edition*, XI, p. 153. The key Freud texts are the 1910 essay 'The Antithetical Meaning of Primary Words', the 1913 'Notes on the Concept of the Unconscious in Psychoanalysis', and the 1925 'Note on the Mystic Writing Pad'. While Derrida has illuminated this modernist, 'written' aspect of Freud's thought, it is important to remember that Freud retained the traditional primacy of spoken language in other texts. In some essays, such as 'The Uncanny', the two concepts of language seem to be operating at the same time, without perceived contradiction. Freud also does not analyse the ambiguous potential of syntax, as Dickinson does.

5. In this light it would be fascinating to compare Dickinson with other modern poets such as Rilke, Tsvetayeva and Berryman (in his sonnets) who are also particularly concerned with the written. Which would be the stronger determinant — sex, the issue of transcendence, or the way the written operates?

6. Probably the modern art work closest to the palimpsest of the Mystic Writing Pad was Kurt Schwitters's 'Merzbau'. Over a period of years Schwitters gradually transformed the interior of his house in Hanover into an accretion of objects, mementoes, inscriptions and images connected with his life. The house was literally Schwitters's capacious container for the personal uncanny. The differences between the 'Merzbau' and the Dickinson poems tell much about fame. Schwitters was inscribing an epic of the trace, a literal life-work of the discontinuous; the first 'Merzbau' was meant to be his monument, but it was destroyed during the Allied fire-bombing of Hanover.

7. Dickinson's practice is more like that of Gwen John, who rarely exhibited her paintings and watercolours, and made no special effort to have them preserved after her death. Other women artists have also shown a comparable craft combined with an apparently odd disregard for the promotion or survival of the work. Elizabeth Bishop revised meticulously and published in the *New Yorker*, but she would neither hurry her collections nor promote them with her personal presence in reading tours. Many women, including Dickinson, 'inscribe' their psychological being on 'magic writing pads' which aren't 'read' by society, such as personal letters and diaries.

Chapter Six: The House Without the Door

1. See Robert Clark, *History, Ideology and Myth in American Fiction 1823–52*, for an account of the pervasiveness of this ideology, even among 'liberal' writers. Clark's account of James Fenimore Cooper's enthusiastic service on behalf of the father is particularly useful. Annette Kolodny's *The Lay of the Land*, covering a longer period, discusses the same appropriative ideology as it exploited the imagery of the land as female.

2. Bryan Jay Wolf has analysed the sense of lassitude and belatedness in early and mid nineteenth-century art in his study *Romantic Re-Vision*. The effort to achieve a heroic sublime resulted in its opposite.

3. See *The Poems and Sonnets of Louise Chandler Moulton*, introduced by Harriet Prescott Spofford, Boston, Little, Brown & Co., 1909.

4. When Dickinson first copied out 'They shut me up in Prose', she wrote that the star would 'Look down upon' captivity. Her revision removes the transcendent connotation of looking down and strengthens the connection between power and language.

5. *Essays and Reviews*, ed. G. R. Thomson, New York, Library of America, 1984, pp. 18–9.

6. *Letters Home: Correspondence 1950–1963*, selected and edited by Aurelia Schober Plath, London, Faber & Faber, 1976, p. 110.

Chapter Seven: An Uncanny Container

1. Ralph Waldo Emerson, *Essays and Lectures*, edited by Joel Porte, New York, Library of America, 1983, p. 126.

2. In his essay, 'The Native Strain: American Orphism', in *Figures of Capable Imagination*, Harold Bloom writes, 'As a heretic from Emersonianism, Dickinson declined to entertain inconsistencies, as her precursor could with his outrageous charm. We can name Emerson accurately as a dozen things . . . we can name Dickinson accurately as only one thing' (p. 83).

3. George Puttenham, *The Arte of English Poesie*, Kent State University Press, 1970 (reprint of A. Constable & Co.'s edition of 1906), p. 193. The complete Oxford English Dictionary cites three similar definitions of metalepsis from rhetorical treatises, the most recent being Hugh Blair's 1783 *Lectures on Rhetoric and Belles Lettres* in an edition of 1812.

4. See Robert Weisbuch, *Emily Dickinson's Poetry*, esp. Chapter 2.
5. See Helen Vendler, *On Extended Wings: Wallace Stevens's Longer Poems*, Cambridge, Mass., Harvard University Press, 1969.
6. Penguin Freud Library, London, 1985, Vol. 14, p. 367.
7. My discussion of Freud's tone and the connection between the uncanny and death is indebted to Hélène Cixous's brilliant article, 'Fiction and Its Phantom: A Reading of Freud's *Das Unheimliche*', New Literary History VII, 3 (Spring 1976), pp. 525–48.

Chapter Eight: The Sister

1. Lists of Dickinson's reading always err on the short side, being limited to books she mentioned by name or quoted. Her true reading was clearly more extensive, but unprovable. Longfellow's romantic novel *Kavanagh* was a youthful favourite, as was the pseudonymous Ik Marvel's *Reveries of a Bachelor*. Among other American writers, she read Hawthorne's tales and *The House of the Seven Gables*; while she doesn't mention *The Scarlet Letter*, it was in the Dickinson library. Her general references to Thoreau indicate close reading, and she seems to have read Melville's *Typee*. Poe she had read, but without enthusiasm. Like everyone else, she absorbed Dickens. She read Wordsworth, Keats, Byron, de Quincey, Robert Browning, Ruskin, Tennyson, Charles Kingsley and, among American poets, William Cullen Bryant, Emerson, Oliver Wendell Holmes and Longfellow. She can also be assumed to have read everything published in the *Atlantic Monthly*, *Scribner's* and the *Springfield Republican*.
2. Bryant's 'The Death of the Flowers' may have been particularly distasteful to Dickinson because it develops from a generalized analogy between flowers and women ('the fair young flowers . . . a beauteous sisterhood') into a use of the seasonal analogy to buttress a smug melancholy over the death of a beautiful young woman. When 'on the hills the golden-rod, and the aster in the wood/. . . in autumn beauty stood' it is appropriate that 'the meek fair blossom' should die: 'And we wept that one so lovely should have a life so brief. . . .'
3. Dickinson's letter inverts the word order of the third line of Wordsworth's stanza:

> Ah! THEN, if mine had been the Painter's hand

> To express what then I saw; and add the gleam,
> The light that never was, on sea or land,
> The consecration, and the Poet's dream.

The full title of Wordsworth's poem is 'Elegiac Stanzas: Suggested by a Picture of Peele Castle, in a Storm, Painted by Sir George Beaumont'. Dickinson attacked the poem again seven years later in a sceptical letter to her cousins, the Norcross sisters (*Letters*, II, p. 510).

4. Ellen Moers, *Literary Women*, Chapters 6, 7 and 8. For Moers 'heroinism' is the woman's perspective, generated by the encounter of female authorial self-consciousness with literary tradition.

5. One of George Eliot's finest poems is a sonnet sequence about her childhood intimacy with her brother, since lost to her with adulthood (furthermore, he cut off contact with her as punishment for her irregular union with Lewes). The quasi-sibling pairing in *Wuthering Heights* is Emily Brontë's female rewriting of the romantic myth of the epipsychidion. Dickinson does have a boy double, called Tim, in one poem, 'We don't cry — Tim and I'.

6. There may be a specific case for the 'witch' association in the case of Elizabeth Barrett Browning, since she was deeply interested in mesmerism and spiritualism. During the 1850s she attended seances. Although spiritualism was not one of Barrett Browning's poetic topics, Dickinson may have picked up hints of a 'magic' personality metaphor. Dickinson herself showed no interest in the popular spiritualism of her day.

7. Dickinson had read Sand's novel *Mauprat*, and perhaps others as well. The quotation in the letter refers to an abridged life of Sand printed in the *Atlantic Monthly*. The best-known self-named and self-crowned figure in the nineteenth century was Napoleon, whom Barrett Browning opposed to the feminine figure of Queen Victoria in the poems 'Crowned and wedded' and 'Crowned and Buried'. Throughout 'Crowned and Buried' it is Napoleon's *name* which is magical. Dickinson used Napoleon's self-crowning/self-naming as symbol for poetic power in 'A little bread — a crust — a crumb', when she writes of the nourished soul being 'Conscious — as old Napoleon,/the might before the Crown!' Emerson also picked up Napoleon's self-crowning, having his American scholar in 'Literary Ethics' paraphrase Napoleon's words upon crowning

himself king of Italy in 1805: 'Please himself with complaisance who will, − for me, things must take my scale, not I theirs. I will say with the warlike king, 'God gave me this crown, and the whole world will not take it away' (*Essays and Lectures*, p. 97).

8. Edmund Clarence Stedman, *The Nature and Elements of Poetry*, Boston and New York, Houghton, Mifflin & Co., 1892, pp. 127−8. Stedman's other contribution to American literature was to include Whitman in his centenary collection of American poetry in 1876, thus signalling Whitman's acceptance by the American literary establishment.

9. Definition from the Oxford English Dictionary. Charles Dickens, describing a young American woman in *American Notes* (1842), remarked: 'The work she had knitted, lay beside her'; Bulwer Lytton, in *A Strange Story* (1862), refers to 'Taking pleasure . . . not in music, nor books, nor that tranquil pastime which women call work' (both also cited in the Oxford English Dictionary). For a fuller account of female expression in weaving and needlework of all kinds, see Roszika Parker, *The Subversive Stitch*, London, The Women's Press, 1984.

10. My reading of 'Sandpiper' is indebted to Seamus Heaney's discussion at the A.E.D.E.A.N. Conference, Murcia, Spain, December 1985.

Chapter Nine: What Emily Knew

1. Allen Ginsberg, 'When the Mode of the Music Changes the Walls of the City Shake', *Poetics of the New American Poetry*, ed. Donald Allen and Warren Tallman, New York, Grove Press, 1973, p. 325.

2. Paul de Man, *Blindness and Insight* (second edition, revised). Minneapolis, University of Minnesota Press, 1983.

BIBLIOGRAPHY

Books by Emily Dickinson

The Complete Poems, (ed.) Johnson, Thomas H., London, Faber & Faber, 1975. (This is the most readily available complete edition.)

The Poems of Emily Dickinson, (ed.) Johnson, Thomas H., Cambridge, Mass., The Belknap Press of Harvard University Press, 1955, 3 volumes.

The Manuscript Books, (ed.) Johnson, Thomas H., Cambridge, Mass., The Belknap Press of Harvard University Press, 1955, 3 volumes.

The Letters, (ed.) Johnson, Thomas H., and Ward, Theodora, Cambridge, Mass., The Belknap Press of Harvard University Press, 1958.

The Lyman Letters: New Light on Emily Dickinson and Her Family, Sewall, Richard B., Amherst, University of Massachusetts Press, 1963.

Books and articles about Emily Dickinson

Baym, Nina, 'God, Father and Lover in Emily Dickinson's Poetry', (ed.) Elliott, Emory, *Puritan Influences in American Literature*, Urbana, University of Illinois Press, 1979, pp. 193–209.

Benfey, Christopher E. G., *Emily Dickinson and the Problem of Others*, Amherst, University of Massachusetts Press, 1984.

Budick, E. Miller, 'Temporal Consciousness and the Perception of Eternity in Emily Dickinson', *Essays in Literature* (USA) 10, Part 2 (Fall 1983), pp. 227–39.

Budick, E. Miller, 'The Dangers of the Living Word: Aspects of Dickinson's Epistemology, Cosmology, and Symbolism', *ESQ* 29 (Fourth Quarter, 1983), pp. 208–24.

Cameron, Sharon, *Lyric Time: Dickinson and the Limits of Genre*, Baltimore, Johns Hopkins University Press, 1979.

Capps, Jack L., *Emily Dickinson's Reading*, Cambridge, Mass., Harvard University Press, 1966.

Cody, John, *After Great Pain*, Cambridge, Mass., Harvard University Press, 1971.

Cuddy, Lois, 'The Influence of Latin Poetics on Emily Dickinson's Style', *Comparative Literature Studies* XIII (1976), pp. 214—29.

Cuddy, Lois, 'The Latin Imprint on Emily Dickinson's Poetry: Theory and Practice', *American Literature* 50 (1978—9), pp. 74—84.

Diehl, Joanne Feit, *Dickinson and the Romantic Imagination*, Princeton, Princeton University Press, 1980.

Diehl, Joanne Feit, ' "Ransom in a Voice": Language as Defense in Dickinson's Poetry', Juhasz, *Feminist Critics Read Emily Dickinson*.

Duchac, Joseph, *The Poems of Emily Dickinson: An Annotated Guide to Commentary Published in English, 1890—1977*. Boston, Mass., G. K. Hall, 1979.

Eberwein, Jane Donahue, *Dickinson: Strategies of Limitation*, Amherst, Mass., University of Massachusetts Press, 1985.

Gelpi, Albert, *Emily Dickinson: The Mind of the Poet*, Cambridge, Harvard University Press, 1965.

Gelpi, Albert, 'Emerson: The Paradox of Organic Form', (ed.) Levin, David, *Emerson*, pp. 149—70.

Gilbert, Sandra, 'The Wayward Nun beneath the Hill: Emily Dickinson and the Mysteries of Womanhood', (ed.) Juhasz, *Feminist Critics Read Emily Dickinson*, pp. 22—44.

Gilbert, Sandra and Gubar, Susan, *The Madwoman in the Attic: The Woman Writer and the Nineteenth Century Literary Imagination*, New Haven and London, Yale University Press, 1979.

Gubar, Susan: see Gilbert, Sandra.

Gubar, Susan, ' "The Blank Page" and the Issues of Female Creativity', *Critical Inquiry* 8, No. 2 (Winter 1981), pp. 243—63 (Special Issue on Writing and Critical Difference).

Hagenbüchle, Roland, 'Precision and Indeterminacy in the Poetry of Emily Dickinson'. *ESQ* No. 20 (1973—74), pp. 70—7.

Hagenbüchle, Roland, 'Sign and Process: The Concept of Language in Emerson and Dickinson', *ESQ* 25 (1974), pp. 137—55.

Homans, Margaret, *Women Writers and Poetic Identity: Dorothy Wordsworth, Emily Brontë, and Emily Dickinson*. Princeton, Princeton University Press, 1980.

Homans, Margaret, ' "Oh, Vision of Language!": Dickinson's Poems of Love and Death', (ed.) Juhasz *Feminist Critics Read Emily Dickinson*, pp. 114—33.

Juhasz, Suzanne, (ed.) *Feminist Critics Read Emily Dickinson*, Bloomington, Indiana University Press, 1983.

Juhasz, Suzanne, *The Undiscovered Continent: Emily Dickinson and the Space of Mind*, Bloomington, Indiana University Press, 1983.

Keller, Karl, *The Only Kangaroo Among the Beauty: Emily Dickinson and America*, Baltimore and London, Johns Hopkins University Press, 1979.

Kher, Inder Nath, *The Landscape of Absence*, New Haven and London, Yale University Press, 1974.

Knox, Helène, 'Metaphor and Metonymy in Emily Dickinson's Figurative Thinking', *Massachusetts Studies in English* VII, 4 and VIII, 1 (1981), pp. 49–56 (double issue on Dickinson).

Leyda, Jay, *The Years and Hours of Emily Dickinson*, New Haven, Yale University Press, 1960.

Lindberg-Seyersted, Brita, *The Voice of the Poet: Aspects of Style in the Poetry of Emily Dickinson*, Cambridge, Mass., Harvard University Press, 1966.

Miller, Christanne, 'How "Low Feet" Stagger: Disruptions of Language in Dickinson's Poetry', (ed.) Juhasz, *Feminist Critics Read Emily Dickinson*, pp. 134–55.

Morris, Adelaide, ' "The Love of Thee – a Prism Be": Men and Women in the Love Poetry of Emily Dickinson', (ed.) Juhasz, *Feminist Critics Read Emily Dickinson*, pp. 98–113.

Mossberg, Barbara Antonina Clarke, *Emily Dickinson: When a Writer is a Daughter*, Bloomington, Indiana University Press, 1982.

Patterson, Rebecca, *The Riddle of Emily Dickinson*, Boston, Houghton Mifflin & Co., 1951.

Patterson, Rebecca, *Emily Dickinson's Imagery*, (ed.) Freeman, Margaret H., Amherst, University of Massachusetts Press, 1979.

Pollak, Vivian R., *Dickinson: The Anxiety of Gender*, Ithaca and London, Cornell University Press, 1984.

Porter, David, *Dickinson: The Modern Idiom*, Cambridge, Mass., and London, Harvard University Press, 1981.

Rich, Adrienne, 'Vesuvius at Home: The Power of Emily Dickinson', *On Lies, Secrets and Silence*, London, Virago Press, 1980.

Sewall, Richard, (ed.) *Emily Dickinson: A Collection of Critical Essays*, Englewood Cliffs, N.J., Prentice-Hall, 1983.

Weisbuch, Robert, *Emily Dickinson's Poetry*, Chicago and London, University of Chicago Press, 1975.

Whicher, George, *This Was a Poet: A Critical Biography of Emily Dickinson*, New York, Scribner's, 1938.

Wolosky, Shira, *Emily Dickinson: A Voice of War*, New Haven and London, Yale University Press, 1984.

Related books and articles

Baym, Nina, *Woman's Fiction: A Guide to Novels by and about Women in America 1820–1870*, Ithaca and London, Cornell University Press, 1978.

Bloom, Harold, *Figures of Capable Imagination*, New York, Seabury Press, 1976.

Bloom, Harold, 'The Freshness of Transformation: Emerson's Dialectics of Influence', (ed.) Levin, David, *Emerson*, pp. 129–48.

Browning, Elizabeth Barrett, *Aurora Leigh*, (ed. and intro.) Kaplan, Cora, London, The Women's Press, 1978.

Chodorow, Nancy, *The Reproduction of Mothering*, Berkeley, University of California Press, 1978.

Cixous, Hélène, 'Fiction and its Phantoms: A Reading of Freud's *Das Unheimliche*', *New Literary History*, VII, 3 (Spring 1976), pp. 525–48.

Clark, Robert, *History, Ideology and Myth in American Fiction, 1823–52*, London, Macmillan, 1984.

Cott, Nancy F., *The Bonds of Womanhood: 'Women's Sphere' in New England 1780–1835*, New Haven, Yale University Press, 1977.

de Man, Paul, *Blindness and Insight: Essays in the Rhetoric of Contemporary Criticism*, Minneapolis, University of Minnesota Press, 1983 (second edition, revised).

Derrida, Jacques, *Writing and Difference*, (trans. and ed.) Bass, Alan, London, Routledge & Kegan Paul, 1978.

Derrida, Jacques, *Of Grammatology*, (trans.) Spivak, Gayatri, Baltimore, Johns Hopkins Press, 1976.

Douglas, Ann, *The Feminization of American Culture*, New York, Alfred A. Knopf, 1977.

Faderman, Lilian, *Surpassing the Love of Men: Love Between Women from the Renaissance to the Present*, New York, Morrow, 1981.

Freud, Sigmund,
    'The Antithetical Meaning of Primal Words' (1910), *Standard Edition*, Vol. 11, pp. 153–61.
    'A Note on the Unconscious in Psychoanalysis' (1912), *Standard Edition*, Vol. 12, pp. 255–67.
    'Instincts and their Vicissitudes' (1915), *Standard Edition*, Vol. 14, pp. 109–40.
    'The "Uncanny"' (1919), *Standard Edition*, Vol. 17, pp. 217–53.
    'Note on the "Mystic Writing Pad" ' (1925 [1924]), *Standard Edition*, Vol. 19, pp. 227–34.

'On the Psychological Consequence of Physiological Difference' (1925) [originally trans. as 'Some Psychical Consequences of Physiological Difference'], *Standard Edition*, Vol. 19, pp. 241–60.

Gilmore, Michael T, *American Romanticism and the Marketplace*, Chicago and London, University of Chicago Press, 1985.

Gonnaud, Maurice, 'Emerson and the Imperial Self: A European Critique', Levin, David, (ed.) *Emerson*, pp. 197–28.

Hyde, Lewis, *The Gift: Imagination and the Erotic Life of Property*, New York, Vintage Books, 1983 (first pub. Random House, 1979).

Hymowitz, Carol and Weisman, Michaele, *A History of Women in America*, New York, Bantam Books, 1978.

Irigaray, Luce, *The Speculum of Other Women*, Ithaca, Cornell University Press, 1985.

Juhasz, Suzanne, *Naked and Fiery Forms: Modern American Poetry by Women, A New Tradition*, New York, Harper & Row, 1976.

Kolodny, Annette, *The Lay of the Land: Metaphor as Experience and History in American Life and Letters*, Chapel Hill, University of North Carolina Press, 1975.

Kristeva, Julia, *Desire in Language: A Semiotic Approach to Literature and Art*, (trans.) Gora, Thomas, Jardine, Alice, and Roudiez, Leon, New York, Columbia University Press, 1980.

Kristeva, Julia, *The Powers of Horror: an Essay on Abjection*, (trans.) Roudiez, Leon, New York, Columbia University Press, 1982.

Lacan, Jacques, *Ecrits: A Selection*, (trans.) Sheridan, Alan, London, Tavistock Publications, 1980 (first published 1977).

Lacan, Jacques, *The Four Fundamental Concepts of Psychoanalysis*, (trans.) Sheridan, Alan, London, The Hogarth Press and the Institute of Psychoanalysis, 1977.

Leitch, Vincent B., *Deconstructive Criticism: An Advanced Introduction*, London, Hutchinson, 1983.

Lerner, Gerda, *The Majority Finds its Past: Placing Women in History*, Oxford and New York, Oxford University Press, 1979.

Levin, David, (ed.) *Emerson: Prophecy, Metamorphosis, and Influence*, New York and London, New York University Press, 1975.

Longworth, Polly, *Austin and Mabel: The Amherst Love Affair and Love Letters of Austin Dickinson and Mabel Loomis Todd*, New York, Farrar, Straus & Giroux, 1984.

Merriam, George S., *The Life and Times of Samuel Bowles*, New York, Da Capo Press, 1970, 2 volumes (reprint of first edition [no publisher given] New York, 1885).

Moers, Ellen, *Literary Women*, London, The Women's Press, 1978.

Porte, Joel, *Representative Man: Ralph Waldo Emerson in His Time*, New York, Oxford University Press, 1979.

Porter, David, *Emerson and Literary Change*, Cambridge, Mass., and London, Harvard University Press, 1978.

Puttenham, George, *The Arte of English Poesie*, Kent State University Press, 1970 (facsimile of the 1906 reprint by A. Constable of the original 1589 edition).

Rich, Adrienne, *Of Woman Born: Motherhood as Experience and Institution*, London, Virago Press, 1977.

Ricoeur, Paul, *The Rule of Metaphor: Multi-disciplinary Studies of the Creation of Meaning in Language*, (trans.) Czerny, Robert, London, Routledge & Kegan Paul, 1978.

Showalter, Elaine, *A Literature of Their Own: British Women Novelists from Brontë to Lessing*, London, Virago Press, 1982 [1977].

Showalter, Elaine, 'Towards a Feminist Poetics', (ed.) Jacobus, Mary, *Women Writing and Writing About Women*, London, Croom Helm, 1979.

Stedman, Edmund Clarence, *The Nature and Elements of Poetry*, Boston and New York, Houghton Mifflin & Co., 1892.

Walker, Cheryl, *The Nightingale's Burden: Women Poets and American Culture before 1900*, Bloomington, Indiana University Press, 1982.

Welter, Barbara, *Divinity Convictions*, Athens, Ohio University Press, 1976.

Wolf, Bryan Jay, *Romantic Re-Vision: Culture and Consciousness in Nineteenth Century American Painting and Literature*, New Haven and London, Yale University Press, 1984.

Yoder, R. A., *Emerson and the Orphic Poet in America*, Berkeley, Los Angeles and London, University of California Press, 1978.

INDEX

FIRST LINES OF POEMS CITED IN TEXT